THE
BIG LIE

THE
BIG LIE

How Our Government

HOODWINKED THE PUBLIC,

Emptied The S.S. Trust Fund,

and caused

The Great
Economic Collapse

Allen W. Smith, Ph.D.
Professor Emeritus Eastern Illinois University

IRONWOOD PUBLICATIONS
Frostproof, Florida

For my wife,

Joan Rugel Smith

and family,

Mark, Jacki, Connor, and Noah

Michael and Dealyne

Lisa, Gary, and Garrett

Grandma Inez W. Smith

Contents

PREFACE

The great economic collapse of 2008 started with the implosion of the American banking system, and then spread, like wildfire, throughout the entire global economy. It happened so fast that the whole world was soon in a state of shock and disbelief. How could things get so bad so fast? Answering that question is the purpose of this book.

For more than a decade, I have been trying to alert the public to the fact that government economic malpractice would almost certainly lead us to such a crisis, if we didn't change course. My book, *The Alleged Budget Surplus, Social Security, and Voodoo Economics,* was published in September 2000, during the heated presidential election campaign. The message of that book was that the proposed economic policies of either George W. Bush or Al Gore would lead to economic disaster if implemented.

On September 27, 2000, I appeared on CNN TODAY with Lou Waters to discuss the newly published book. Excerpts from the transcript of that interview are reproduced below:

CNN Today:

Economist Allen Smith Discusses 'The Alleged Budget Surplus, Social Security & Voodoo Economics'

Aired September 27, 2000 - 2:01 p.m. ET

LOU WATERS, CNN ANCHOR: ...The person you're about to meet might accuse the federal government of economic malpractice. He is economist Allen Smith, who says there is no surplus, that it's all a big, fat myth. His book is entitled "The Alleged Budget Surplus, Social Security & Voodoo Economics."

Dr. Smith joins us from Ft. Myers, Florida. He taught economics for 30 years, retiring from Eastern Illinois University in 1998 to write. And he wrote this book entitled, once again, "The Alleged Budget Surplus, Social Security & Voodoo Economics," all of which suggests you're not elated over President Clinton's announcement today of 19 billion more in the surplus since June.

ALLEN SMITH, AUTHOR, "THE ALLEGED BUDGET SURPLUS, SOCIAL SECURITY & VOODOO ECONOMICS": The figures released today I haven't seen, the breakdown in terms of the amount that is off budget and the amount that is on budget. But like all the other surpluses they've been talking about, most of this is Social Security money and Social Security Trust Fund. Prior to the figures released today, in the last 40 years, we had a surplus in the operating budget of seven-tenths of a billion, or 700 million, and that came in fiscal '99. Thirty-eight years prior to that, every year had a deficit in operating budget. This is Social Security money they're talking about and not general tax revenue.

WATERS: You're saying that this money that we're hearing is a government surplus that we're paying down the federal debt with is Social Security money?

SMITH: It is Social Security money, and they are not paying down the national debt...

WATERS: Well, if what you say is true, what do we make of these political promises of a prescription drug benefit, preschool for all, college tuition paid for, tax cuts? We heard Al Gore just a few minutes ago saying they, meaning Republicans, would squander the surpluses. And he's talking about a tax cut.

SMITH: These are outrageous proposals, both the proposals of George W. Bush and that of Al Gore, will tend to derail the economy, as has happened so many times before. I don't know if they've consulted with any economists, if they've looked at the facts. But Al Gore has said we'll be debt-free by 2012, and you can— anybody can go to the Internet and get this "Mid-Session Review." It's from the office of the president, the OMB, submitted to Congress in June. And the figures in here will show that President Clinton is showing an increase in the national debt between 2000 and 2012 of about close to an additional trillion dollars.

WATERS: So we're being misled by the politicians with all these campaign promises?

SMITH: We are being totally deceived. I think this is the biggest deception in American history...

WATERS: Is there a danger for the future?

SMITH: There is a big danger because our economy right now is healthy, extremely healthy, but the budget of the United States government is probably the worst it's ever been in terms of indebtedness, and any actions taken by the government does have an impact on the economy. And I think that either—the plans of either of the two candidates will derail this economy and put us back into recession and major problems...

WATERS: A dire warning from economist Allen Smith. Thank you, Professor, for joining us today.

SMITH: Thank you for having me.

WATERS: The book: "The Alleged Budget Surplus, Social Security & Voodoo Economics."

Even as I spoke during that interview, the seeds that would yield the terrible harvest of 2008 continued to be sowed. President Clinton had cooperated with Congressional Republicans the previous year in repealing the Glass-Steagall Act of 1933, a primary pillar of FDR's New Deal legislation that was designed to prevent a repeat of the 1930s financial collapse. When President Clinton signed into law the bill that repealed the Glass-Steagall Act, on November 12, 1999, he opened the floodgates for mass mergers of companies in the financial industries. In 2000, by creating the budget-surplus myth, Clinton was unwittingly laying the foundation for George W. Bush's devastating tax cuts. Those tax cuts, along with the deregulation of the banking industry, started the clock that would continue to tick until the Wall Street meltdown.

CHAPTER ONE

Blueprint for Economic Disaster

The Wall Street meltdown of 2008, and the global economic collapse that followed, were not acts of God. They were not natural disasters, and they were not inevitable. They were man-made, and they should never have been allowed to happen. The United States of America had been gradually heading toward economic crises for a full quarter-century, ever since Ronald Reagan abandoned traditional economic policies in 1981 and launched the nation in a dangerous new direction.

On February 18, 1981, President Ronald Reagan delivered to a cheering joint session of Congress and a prime-time television audience a speech that marked a sharp turning point in American history. His "Program for Economic Recovery" represented a radical departure from the political and economic thinking that had dominated the American government for the past 40 years.

Among other things, President Reagan called for passage of the controversial Kemp-Roth tax cut proposal that would cut personal income tax rates by 30 percent over a three-year period. As *Newsweek* magazine put it in its March 2, 1981 issue, "Reagan thus gambled the future—his own, his party's, and in some measure the nation's—on a perilous and largely untested new course called supply-side economics." In addition to his tax-cutting policies, Ronald Reagan was a strong advocate of reducing the role of government in the economy. One of his favorite lines was, "Government is not the solution, government is the problem."

Reagan saw big government as an evil, and he saw big business as a virtue. He had despised the government regulation and increased spending that had taken place during the Roosevelt era and during the presidencies of John F. Kennedy and Lyndon B. Johnson.

Reagan had an enormous impact on the thinking of the American people in terms of the proper role of government. He stirred up the greatest opposition to taxes since the Boston Tea Party. He convinced many that high federal taxes were an evil to be avoided at all costs, and he implemented huge tax cuts without any specific plans to reduce government spending. He even argued that lower tax rates would yield increased tax revenue because of a magic ingredient in his new supply-side economic theories.

Essentially, Reagan switched the federal government from what he critically called a "tax and spend" policy to a "borrow and spend" policy, where the government continued its heavy spending but used borrowed money instead of tax revenue to pay the bills. The results were catastrophic. Although it had taken this nation more than 200 years to accumulate the first $1 trillion of national debt, during the 12 years of the Reagan-Bush administrations, that debt quadrupled to $4 trillion!

President Reagan's proposed 30 percent cut in tax rates over a three-year period was based on the argument that such a tax cut would result in a substantial increase in the total supply of goods and services produced. The argument was based on the belief that tax rates were so high that many individuals took more lengthy vacations, accepted less overtime work, and retired earlier than they would if tax rates were substantially lower. In addition, the supply-siders argued that the high tax rates discouraged business people from pursuing promising but risky investment opportunities because even if they were successful the government would take much of the profits in higher taxes.

These beliefs led supply-siders to argue that a massive tax cut, such as Reagan's proposal for a 30 percent cut in tax rates over a three-year period, would lead to more revenue, not less. The American people were told that they could have their cake and eat it too, and they loved it. According to Reagan, he could cut tax rates by 30 percent and collect more revenue than before the tax cut. In fact, President Reagan promised that if Congress would just enact his proposal, the federal budget would be balanced by 1984 and he would simultaneously reduce both unemployment and inflation.

Congress did enact the President's economic program, including the tax-cut proposal, which had been reduced (at the request of Budget Director David Stockman) from a 30 percent cut to a 25 percent cut in personal income tax rates over a three-year period. However, the country soon learned that the promised simultaneous reduction in inflation and unemployment was not to be.   Inflation did come down, as the economy plunged into the worst recession in half a century.   The civilian unemployment rate climbed to 10.7 percent in December 1982, the highest since the Great Depression of the 1930s.   Millions of Americans lost their jobs, and the annual civilian unemployment rate remained above 9.5 percent for both 1982 and 1983.

As the economy recovered from the severe recession, President Reagan argued that his economic policies were working and the economy was headed toward true and lasting prosperity.   On the surface things did look encouraging.   The unemployment rate was gradually declining, and inflation was remaining low.   However, a huge, dark cloud hung over the optimism because of the unprecedented size of the federal budget deficits and the rapid growth in the national debt.

A president, who had promised that his policies would lead to a balanced budget by 1984, instead gave us record budget deficits and a doubling of the national debt in five years.   The federal budget deficits soared from $73.8 billion in fiscal 1980 to a record $237.9 billion in fiscal 1986.

Nations, like individuals, cannot indefinitely live beyond their means.   While much of the borrowed money came from Americans who invested in government securities, substantial amounts of foreign capital was used to finance the huge budget deficits. This practice of borrowing from foreigners was the beginning of a trend that would become a cause for alarm more than two decades later when the bottom fell out of the world financial system.

Why were the basic economic problems allowed to grow to such disastrous proportions? The primary reason was that, for the first time in modern history, an American president chose to almost totally ignore the advice of professional economists, both inside and outside of the administration. Unless an economist could be found whose advice was compatible with Ronald Reagan's economic and political views, the administration simply ignored the advice. It would have been bad enough if the President had just ignored the advice of outside economists and had listened to his own handpicked economists. However, he ignored both groups.

When Murray Weidenbaum, Reagan's first Chairman of the Council of Economic Advisers, resigned early in the administration, the President had the opportunity to search the nation for his type of economist as Weidenbaum's replacement. Finally, in 1982, he selected Martin Feldstein, a Harvard economist, as his new Chairman.

Mr. Feldstein took his appointment seriously, and he expected to influence economic policy within the administration. He immediately began to warn the President about the gigantic federal budget deficits and insisted that something be done to reduce them. However, Feldstein soon learned that he had been appointed only to fill the position, and that his advice was not going to be taken seriously.

When Feldstein warned of the deficit dangers in the annual Economic Report of the President, Treasury Secretary, Donald Regan, a non-economist who was playing a major role in economic policy making, told Congress, "As far as I'm concerned, you can throw it (The Economic Report) away."

Feldstein had warned that the deficits, if not cur-
tailed soon, could devastate the nation's economy.
Feldstein had argued that taxes should be raised as a
way of reducing the projected $180 billion fiscal
1985 deficit. (As it turned out, the actual on-budget
deficit for fiscal 1985 was $221.5 billion.)

When, out of frustration, Feldstein began giving
public speeches on the subject of the dangerous
deficits, he was ordered to submit his speeches to
the White House for prior approval before giving
them. The final straw fell when, just a short time
before Feldstein was scheduled to appear on an
ABC news show on Sunday February 5, 1984, he
was ordered by the White House to cancel the
scheduled appearance because his comments might
embarrass the administration.

Usually, new economic theories require years of
debate and testing before they stand a chance of being implemented as a part of government economic
policy, even when they are the product of some of
the greatest minds in the field. But, because the
ideas of the supply-side supporters were so compatible with the political philosophy of Ronald
Reagan, the new, untested theory was to become the
cornerstone of Reagan's economic policy.

With the benefit of hindsight, we can now clearly
see that it was a blueprint for economic disaster.
Even if the flawed policies had ended for good after
the 12 years of Reagan-Bush, the nation would have
been negatively affected for years to come. But,
after an eight-year return to traditional economic
policies under President Clinton, George W. Bush
reinstated Reaganomics and completed the nation's
journey to economic disaster.

Even before the Reagan administration had implemented any of its economic policies, Americans were warned of the dangers inherent in Reagan's proposals by economists. Paul Samuelson, the first American to receive the coveted Nobel Prize in economics, was one of the first well-known economists to warn of the dire consequences that would result if Reagan's proposals were put into effect. Samuelson, who wrote a regular column for *Newsweek* at the time, had access to a mass audience, and he warned the public of the dangers inherent in Reagan's economic proposals. Below is an excerpt from an article by Samuelson that appeared in the March 2, 1981 issue of *Newsweek*.

> Reagan's program does attempt a radical break with the past. A radical-right crusade is being sold as a solution for an economy allegedly in crisis. There is no such crisis! Our people should join this crusade only if they agree with its philosophical conservative merits. They should not be flim-flammed by implausible promises that programs to restore the 1920s' inequalities will cure the inflation problem.

Dr. Samuelson did everything within his power to alert America to the dangers it was facing. But it was to no avail. His warnings fell mostly on deaf ears. Very few Americans cared about what professional economists thought, even Nobel prize-winning economists. They believed whatever the charismatic Reagan told them. He had promised that he could deliver a major tax cut and still balance the budget by 1984. Why should the people take the word of Samuelson over that of the President who had just been elected by a landslide? Never mind that Reagan chose a 34-year-old with no training in economics as one of his two top economic policy makers, or that he ignored the advice of his own Council of Economic Advisers. Surely the President knew what he was doing.

Reagan's primary economic policy makers in the early years of the administration were Treasury Secretary, Donald Regan, and Budget Director, David Stockman. Mr. Regan, who was the former head of the Merrill Lynch stock brokerage firm, had business experience, but he was not an economist. Budget Director, David Stockman, had absolutely no formal training in economics. Yet despite the warnings of many outside prominent economists, as well as his own hand-picked Harvard economist, Martin Feldstein, President Reagan allowed these non-economists to formulate national economic policy.

Much was learned about the early days of the Reagan Administration with the publication of the infamous article, "The Education of David Stockman" by William Greider in the December 1981 issue of *The Atlantic Monthly*. When Stockman's appointment as budget director first seemed likely, he had agreed to meet with William Greider, an assistant managing editor at the *Washington Post*, from time to time and relate, off the record, his private account of the great political struggle ahead. The particulars of these conversations were not to be reported until later, after the President's program had been approved by Congress. Stockman and Greider met for regular conversations over breakfast for eight months, and these conversations provided the basis for Greider's article in *The Atlantic Monthly*.

When the article was published, it became a political bombshell. In addition to the revelation that Stockman had rigged the computer at OMB in order to get budget projections that could be sold to the Congress, Stockman asserted that the supply-side theory was not a new economic theory at all but just new language and argument for the doctrine of the old Republican orthodoxy known as "trickle down" economics. Basically, this doctrine holds that the government should give tax cuts to the top brackets; the wealthiest individuals and the largest enterprises, and let the good effects "trickle down" through the economy to reach everyone else.

According to Stockman, when one stripped away the new rhetoric emphasizing across-the-board cuts, the supply-side theory was really new clothes for the unpopular doctrine of the old Republican orthodoxy. Stockman said, "It's kind of hard to sell 'trickle down,' so the supply-side formula was the only way to get a tax policy that was really 'trickle down.' Supply-side is 'trickle down' theory."

Stockman said that the Kemp-Roth tax cut bill was a Trojan horse to bring down the top rate. "The hard part of the supply-side tax cut is dropping the top rate from 73 to 50 percent—the rest of it is a secondary matter," Stockman said. "The original argument was that the top bracket was too high, and that's having the most devastating effect on the economy. Then, the general argument was that, in order to make this palatable as a political matter, you had to bring down all brackets. But, I mean, Kemp-Roth was always a Trojan horse to bring down the top rate."

A primary goal of the Reagan tax cuts was to reduce government spending. He thought that, if less revenue was available, there would have to be sharp reductions in spending. However, instead of cutting spending, Congress simply borrowed the money to replace the revenue lost from the tax cut.

Reagan said over and over that the economic problems of America were the result of too much government. He wanted to trim the size of the federal government as much as possible, and he seemed to believe that if taxes were cut severely, there would be a corresponding cut in federal spending. In Reagan's first inaugural address he said,

> "...great as our tax burden is, it has not kept pace with public spending. For decades, we have piled deficit upon deficit, mortgaging our future and our children's future for the temporary convenience of the present. To continue this long trend is to guarantee tremendous social, cultural, political, and economic upheavals.
>
> You and I, as individuals, can, by borrowing, live beyond our means, but for only a limited period of time. Why, then, should we think that collectively, as a nation, we are not bound by that same limitation?
>
> ...It is my intention to curb the size and influence of the Federal establishment and to demand recognition of the distinction between the powers granted to the Federal Government and those reserved to the States or to the people...It is no coincidence that our present troubles parallel and are proportionate to the intervention and intrusion in our lives that result from unnecessary and excessive growth of government."

We can now see just how contradictory Reagan's words and actions were. When he said, "For decades, we have piled deficit upon deficit, mortgaging our future and our children's future for the temporary convenience of the present," a reasonable person would likely conclude that Reagan was being critical of large government deficits. One would then further conclude that Reagan intended to follow policies that would result in smaller deficits than in the past. Instead, Reagan gave us budget deficits of a magnitude not even imaginable in the past.

Prior to Reagan's presidency, we had never had a budget deficit as high as $100 billion, and only two years with deficits in the $70 billion range. In 1976, during the Ford administration, the deficit was $70.5 billion. In 1980, during the Carter administration, the deficit was $72.2 billion. Both of these deficits were primarily the result of economic recessions that reduced the government's tax revenue. The average annual deficit for the entire decade of the 1970s was only $35.38 billion. These are the deficits that Reagan was so critical of—the ones he said had mortgaged our future and our children's future."

The average deficit of $168.87 billion for the entire decade of the 1980s dwarfed that for the decade of the 1970s. The annual deficits soared under both President Reagan and President George Herbert Walker Bush. The 1982 deficit of $120.1 billion represented the first time in history that the deficit had topped the $100 billion mark. The very next year, in 1983, the deficit exceeded the $200 billion mark, weighing in at $207.7 billion.

The longer the Reagan economic policies were in place, the larger the budget deficits became. In 1992, the last year of the George H.W. Bush administration, the budget deficit was an astronomical $340.4 billion! The national debt, which was less than $1 trillion when Reagan assumed the presidency, was more than $4 trillion by the time Bush turned over the reigns of power to Bill Clinton.

If we look at Mr. Reagan's full 8-year presidency, the average annual unemployment rate is 7.5 percent. Since the Great Depression, only in 1975 and 1976, during the Ford presidency, has the unemployment rate been as high, in even a single year, as Reagan's 8-year average unemployment rate.

As Reagan's vice president, George Herbert Walker Bush inherited enough goodwill from his association with Reagan to get elected to a first term. However, Bush lacked Reagan's charisma and was on probation with the American voters from the day he took office. If he were to have any chance of being reelected to a second term, he would have to turn the economy around. And, given the fact that he had referred to Reagan's economic proposals as "voodoo economics" that would lead to disaster, during the 1980 primaries, many observers hoped that Bush would abandon Reaganomics and return to more traditional economic policies. But Bush continued with the same failed economic policies that had done so much harm to the econmy and the federal budget under Reagan.

Bush's failure to chart a new course, with regard to economic policies, cost him reelection. Although Bush was riding so high in the public opinion polls after the Gulf War that most of the strongest Democratic potential challengers chose not to even run, Bush's poor handling of the economy caused him to lose the Presidency to a little-known governor from Arkansas, Bill Clinton.

Between 1981 and 1986, the United States was transformed from the world's largest lender to the world's largest borrower. Although most Americans were never made aware of this historic role reversal for the United States, we can be sure that our adversaries around the world took note of it. At the very same time that President Ronald Reagan was building up our military strength to enhance our security and status in the world, our economic strength was waning as we saw our role as the world's largest lender being replaced with the dubious distinction of being the world's largest borrower.

One might have expected our leaders to be so concerned about America's new status as the world's largest borrower, that they would have put a high priority on taking actions that would help undo the role reversal. But they were not. They seemed to be comfortable with their "borrow and spend" approach to handling the government's finances.

The 1984 presidential election campaign showed just how naïve, and economically illiterate the American electorate is. It also demonstrated how a charismatic leader, like Ronald Reagan, can convince the masses to ignore facts, and the advice of experts, and persuade them to follow him wherever he leads, even if it is over the edge of a cliff.

During the 1980 campaign, Reagan had promised that his large tax cuts would lead to a balanced budget by 1984. Instead, the 1984 budget had a deficit of $185.3 billion. Furthermore, the national debt, which had taken 200 years to reach the $1 trillion mark, had increased to $1.56 trillion by 1984, and it was racing toward the $2 trillion mark.

The budget was so out of control that almost every mainstream economist in the country would probably have argued that the 1981 tax cuts were too big and had to be adjusted. Economic advisers to former Vice President Walter Mondale, who was the Democratic presidential nominee in 1984, convinced Mondale that a tax increase was absolutely necessary to bring the runaway deficits under control.

Mondale apparently thought he could be honest with the American people about the deficit problem and the need for a special deficit reduction tax. So Mondale told the voters that a tax increase was inevitable, no matter whether he or Reagan was elected. Mondale said,

> "Mr. Reagan will raise your taxes and so will I. He won't tell you, I just did."

Although he pledged that every dollar of the revenue from the proposed new tax would be used to reduce the deficit, and not a single dollar of it would be used for new spending, Mondale's honesty turned out to be a disastrous strategy. Reagan ridiculed Mondale's tax proposal and promised that he would bring prosperity and balanced budgets without raising taxes.

One might think that, since Reagan had not kept his 1980 promises, and since the runaway deficits were alarming economists and many others, the voters might have been hesitant to vote for Reagan again. But they were not. On election day, Reagan won 49 states, and Mondale won his home state of Minnesota by only 3,800 votes! It was one of the most lopsided landslide victories in history. Historians may eventually decide that it was also one of the greatest mistakes the American people, as a whole, had ever made.

America was on the wrong track in 1984. After 200 years of following reasonably responsible fiscal policies, that had made America the economic envy of the world, the nation had gone on a four-year fling with deficit financing. Instead of living within our means as a nation, we were following a policy of borrowing from future generations in order to spend more than we could afford. It should have been clear to almost everyone that the United States government could not go on, indefinitely, spending more than its income. But apparently it was not.

The 1984 election offered the opportunity for an informed electorate to change the course of history for the better through the democratic process. If the public had been educated in economics, they would have realized that Reagan's flirtation with supply-side economic theory had been disastrous. The supply-side theory had been tested, and it had flunked the test miserably. But America did not have an informed electorate. The public was economically illiterate.

In addition to all the other malpractice during the Reagan-Bush years, it was during this period that the fraudulent use of Social Security surplus revenue for general government funding began. The

1983 Social Security payroll tax increase, which will be described in detail in Chapter Three, began generating surplus Social Security revenue during Reagan's second term.

The planned surpluses, that were supposed to be saved and invested in order to fund the retirement of the baby boomers, started out small but escalated rapidly. Although only about $84.5 billion of Social Security surplus came in during the Reagan presidency, during the four years of George H.W. Bush's presidency, there was an additional $211.7 billion in Social Security surplus revenue. Every penny of the surplus from both the Reagan and Bush administrations was spent on non-Social Security programs.

The surplus money should have been saved and invested. Instead, the surplus Social Security revenue was spent just as if it were general revenue. Bush who had said, during the campaign, "Read my lips. No new taxes," did not need to raise taxes when he could spend money from the Social Security surplus at will.

A few courageous United States Senators tried to nip the Social Security fraud in the bud early on by speaking out against it. The three most vocal senators on the issue were Senator Daniel Patrick Moynihan (D-NY), Senator Ernest (Fritz) Hollings (D-SC), and Senator Harry Reid (D-NV).

On October 13, 1989, Senator Hollings lambasted the Bush administration for its use of Social Security surplus dollars for funding other programs. Excerpts from that speech are reproduced below from the Congressional Record {Page: S13411}.

"...The most reprehensible fraud in this great jam-balaya of frauds is the systematic and total ransacking of the Social Security trust fund in order to mask the true size of the deficit...The public fully supported enactment of hefty new Social Security taxes in 1983 to ensure the retirement program's long-term solvency and credibility. The promise was that today's huge surpluses would be set safely aside in a trust fund to provide for the baby-boomer retirees in the next century.

Well, look again. The Treasury is siphoning off every dollar of the Social Security surplus to meet current operating expenses of the Government...

The hard fact is that, in the next century, the Social Security system will find itself paying out vastly more in benefits than it is taking in through payroll taxes. And the American people will wake up to the reality that those IOU's in the trust fund vault are a 21st century version of Confederate banknotes."

Nearly a year later, the looting of the trust fund was continuing unchanged. On October 9, 1990, Senator Harry Reid expressed his outrage at the practice during a senate speech. Excerpts from the speech are reproduced below from the Congressional Record {Page: S14759}.

"The discussion is are we as a country violating a trust by spending Social Security trust fund moneys for some purpose other than for which they were intended. The obvious answer is yes...

The trust funds resources are there for the well-being of those who have paid into the Social Security System. We should use those resources to see that Social Security recipients are treated well but also treated fairly and treated equitably.

It is time for Congress, I think, to take its hands—and I add the President in on that—off the Social Security surpluses. Stop hiding the horrible truth of the fis-

cal irresponsibility that we have talked about here the
past 2 weeks. It is time to return those dollars to the
hands of those who earned them—the Social Security
beneficiaries and future beneficiaries...

...I think that is a very good illustration of what I
was talking about, embezzlement, thievery. Because
that, Mr. President, is what we are talking about
here...On that chart in emblazoned red letters is what
has been taking place here, embezzlement. During the
period of growth we have had during the past 10 years,
the growth has been from two sources: One, a large
credit card with no limits on it, and, two, we have been
stealing money from the Social Security recipients of
this country.

Out of this heated debate on the issue of government misappropriation of Social Security money,
came Senator Daniel Patrick Moynihan's proposal to
cut Social Security taxes in order to deny the government access to the tempting surplus Social Security money. Senator Moynihan, who had been a
strong supporter of the 1983 efforts to strengthen the
Social Security system, was outraged that, instead of
being used to build up the size of the Social Security
Trust Fund for future retirees as was intended, the
Social Security surplus was being used to pay for
general government spending.

Because Moynihan believed the American
people were being deceived and betrayed, he
proposed undoing the 1983 legislation by cutting
Social Security taxes and returning the system to a
"pay-as-you-go" basis which would have provided
only enough revenue to take care of current retirees.
Moynihan's position was that if the government
could not keep its hands out of the Social Security
cookie jar, the jar should be emptied so there would
be no Social Security surplus.

President George H.W. Bush was furious over Moynihan's proposal. In response to reporters' questions, Bush replied, "It is an effort to get me to raise taxes on the American people by the charade of cutting them, or cut benefits, and I am not going to do it to the older people of this country."

But President Bush was in fact taking money from a fund that was supposed to be used to provide for "the older people of this country" and using it to fund general government. Since none of the $211.7 billion borrowed from Social Security by the Bush administration was repaid during the Bush presidency, higher taxes will have to be levied against the American people at some point in the future if this debt is ever to be repaid.

Despite the strong efforts, way back in 1990, to put an end to the raiding of the Social Security trust fund, President George H.W. Bush continued to loot and spend every dollar of the Social Security surplus.

Even though Social Security funds are required by federal law to be kept separate from other funds, Presidents Reagan and George H.W. Bush treated them just like general revenue, and spent every dollar on other government programs. We would like to think that our two-party system would have eliminated the practice whenever the next Democratic president entered the White House. But it didn't. President Clinton seemed to think that if his two predecessors had gotten by with violating the law and treating the Social Security surpluses as general revenue, then he could probably get by with it too. And he did.

During the 2000 presidential election campaign, both Al Gore and George W. Bush publicly acknowledged the past looting of Social Security money, and they both pledged to end the practice. But George W. Bush blatantly ignored both his pledge and federal law and continued the looting just like his three predecessors.   Almost two decades have passed since Senators Moynihan, Hollings, Reid, and others tried so gallantly to protect the Social Security contributions of American workers, and the practice continues. Back then, the amount of money that was supposed to be in the trust fund was not all that substantial. Today, we are talking about $2.4 trillion in accumulated surpluses that is supposed to be safely locked up in the trust fund. Sadly, there is not a single dollar of real money or any other kind of real asset in the trust fund. It contains only government IOUs that serve as accounting records of how much money the government has taken from Social Security and spent for other purposes.

The American people hear over and over from government officials that the Social Security money has been invested in government bonds. That is a **BIG LIE**. The money is not invested in anything, because it has already been spent. Money can be saved and invested, or it can be spent. However, money cannot be both spent and invested. Once the money is spent, there is nothing left to invest.

The way the government has been able to deceive the public on this issue is through accounting gimmickry. The government created a special type of certificate available only to the trust funds. The certificates are called "special issue

Treasuries" or "special issue Treasury bonds." But
they are not real bonds in the sense that most people
use the term. They are simply accounting devices
for keeping track of how much money the
government owes to Social Security. They are
nothing more than IOUs.

In a Washington speech on January 21, 2005,
David Walker, Comptroller General of the GAO,
sought to make it clear once and for all that the
Social Security trust fund contains no real assets.
He said,

> "There are no stocks or bonds or real estate in the trust
> fund. It has nothing of real value to draw down."

If the trust fund held regular public issue Treasury bonds like everyone else invests in, there would
be no problem. The bonds could be sold in the open
market at any time for full market value. The trust
fund is allowed to hold such bonds and has held
some public issue Treasury bonds in the past.
However, it does not now hold any such bonds.

The special issue certificates are not marketable
and thus cannot be bought or sold for even a penny
on the dollar. They are totally worthless accounting
devices. During President George W. Bush's campaign to partially privatize Social Security, he became desperate to find new ammunition with which
to convince the public that Social Security faces real
problems. Finally, he decided to tell the truth about
the trust fund.

During a speech in Pennsylvania on February 10,
2005, President Bush made a very candid statement
about government Social Security practices. He
said,

"Every dime that goes in from payroll taxes is spent. It's spent on retirees, and if there's excess, it's spent on government programs. The only thing that Social Security has is a pile of IOUs from one part of government to the next."

During a speech in West Virginia on April 5, 2005, President bush said,

"There is no trust fund, just IOUs that I saw first-hand that future generations will pay—will pay for either in higher taxes, or reduced benefits, or cuts to other critical government programs."

Despite these definitive statements by the President and the Comptroller General, we are still being told that all Social Security surplus money is safe and sound because it is invested in "government bonds." In later chapters, I will explain, in detail, why this is not true.

CHAPTER TWO

The Budget-Surplus Myth

Much of the 2000 presidential election campaign revolved around the claim that the United States government had huge budget surpluses that would continue for years to come. This claim was the basis for George W. Bush's promise to cut taxes by $1.3 trillion over the next ten years. It was the reason that Al Gore was able to promise that he would cut taxes, increase spending on education, and pay down a substantial portion of the national debt. This claim was reported to the public as the gospel truth, and almost everyone believed it. There was only one problem. It was all a **BIG LIE**. In terms of indebtedness, the federal government's financial condition was worse in 2000 than it had ever been before.

There is no mystery as to where the public got the idea that the government had somehow stumbled onto a gigantic windfall of excess money. They had been told this over and over by President Clinton and by both presidential candidates. Bill Clinton, Al Gore, and George W. Bush all participated in what was one of the greatest deceptions ever perpetrated on the American people.

Why would President Clinton, Al Gore, George W. Bush, and a host of other politicians from both parties, deliberately mislead the American people on such a crucial matter? The only plausible explanation is that they were trying to convince the people that a surplus existed because the surplus myth fit well into the political agendas of all three.

President Clinton and Vice President Gore wanted a budget surplus to exist so that they could claim that the Clinton Administration, which inherited massive budget deficits, eliminated the deficits and transformed them into large surpluses in just eight years. George W. Bush wanted a surplus to exist so that he could promise major tax cuts and attempt to get to the White House riding the same horse that carried Ronald Reagan to the Oval Office.

The existence of a real budget surplus was in the best interest of both political parties, and the voters loved the idea that the government had become so rich that it could give money back to the people. It was like believing in Santa Claus. All parties had such a strong desire for a real surplus to exist that they pretended that such a surplus actually did exist. But there was no "real" budget surplus in any meaningful sense of the term!

Funds flowing into and out of the Social Security trust fund are by law supposed to be kept separate from other government expenditures. So the government would have a real surplus only if its total spending for everything, except Social Security benefits, was less than its total revenue from all sources, except Social Security payroll taxes. There had been only two years in the past 40 years in which that condition was met. The other 38 years were all deficit years.

There was a tiny $1.9 billion surplus in 1999 and a more substantial $86.4 billion surplus in 2000, at a time when the economy was operating at the peak of the business cycle, and the unemployment rate was at a 30-year low. That's it! These were the only two annual surpluses in the government's operating budget during the previous 40 years. Furthermore, Clinton had run more than $1 trillion in deficits during the preceding six years, and ran an average annual deficit of more the $125 billion per year during his entire eight years as president.

The surpluses that everyone was talking about in 2000 were "projected" surpluses. They were figments of President Clinton's imagination. The planned Social Security Trust Fund surplus, that was off budget and earmarked for funding the baby boomers' retirement, first became large enough to more than offset the continuing on-budget deficit in 1998, a year in which there was a $30 billion deficit in the operating budget. Instead of reporting the actual deficit of $30 billion, Clinton announced a $69.2 billion federal budget surplus for 1998. Clinton simply took the $99.2 billion Social Security surplus for that year, and subtracted the on-budget deficit of $30 billion to arrive at the mythical figure of a $69.2 billion surplus for 1998.

Despite the fact that the $1.9 billion surplus for 1999 was the first on-budget federal surplus in 38 years, Clinton was not content to just report the real surplus to the public. Instead, he added the $123.7

billion Social Security surplus for 1999 to the $1.9 billion real surplus and reported the combined total to the American public as the actual surplus. Finally, in fiscal 2000, Clinton added the $149.8 billion Social Security surplus to the $86.4 billion real surplus and reported a whopping surplus of more than $230 billion.

Clinton's true record of deficit reduction would have been phenomenal if he had just been honest with the public, and the Budget Enforcement Act of 1990 prohibited Clinton from legally combining the Social Security and non-Social Security budgets for purposes of reporting deficits or surpluses. But Clinton chose to violate federal law and deceive the American people with regard to the true status of the budget.

When Clinton assumed the presidency in 1993, after twelve years of reckless Reaganomics, the nation was near the brink of economic calamity. However, by 2000, eight years of sound economic policies had brought the nation to a crucial new fork in the road. One option was to continue down the Clinton road and begin to pay down the national debt that had risen so much in the previous 20 years.

The alternative was to take the fork in the road that led to a new round of Reaganomics with huge budget deficits and a skyrocketing national debt. It was clear that George W. Bush would give us a new round of Reaganomics. However, it wasn't totally clear that Al Gore would give us a continuation of the Clinton policies. Like Bush's proposals, Gore's promised tax cuts and new spending were based on the assumption that the fantasy projected budget surpluses were real. Unfortunately, they were not real.

The circumstances that made it possible for Clinton, Gore, and Bush to pull the wool over the eyes of the public in 2000 dated back to the Social Security Amendments of 1983. These amendments were enacted to improve the solvency of the Social Security Trust Fund that had run small budget deficits for seven years in a row from 1976 through 1982.

The legislation was designed so the increased payroll taxes would generate annual Social Security surpluses each and every year until 2017. However, the surpluses would come to an end that year, and the Social Security fund would experience deficits from that point on. The plan was to build up a large enough reserve in the trust fund by 2017 to fund the payment of full Social Security benefits during the years 2018 to 2042, at which time the youngest of the baby boomers would be 77 years old. The surplus Social Security money was to be saved and invested, and it was specifically earmarked for the payment of retirement benefits for the baby boomers.

The new legislation generated a Social Security surplus of $9.4 billion in 1985 with increasingly larger yearly surpluses thereafter. The Social Security surplus was $38.8 billion in 1988, $56.6 billion in 1990, and $99.2 billion in 1998. It was the 1998 Social Security surplus of $99.2 billion that paved the way for the budget surplus myth. .

The government ran a deficit of $30.0 billion in its operating budget in 1998. However, since the Social Security surplus was larger than the operating-budget deficit for the first time ever, President

Clinton took a giant leap into fantasyland and announced that the government had a surplus of $69.2 billion, the first surplus since the Vietnam War.

As mentioned above, Clinton also added the Social Security surpluses to the real budget surpluses of the next two years, greatly inflating their true size. The American people were primed to accept even more good news about government surplus money, and Clinton was ready to accommodate them.

It would have been bad enough if this had been the extent of Clinton's accounting mischief. But this was only the beginning. Clinton claimed that the budget surpluses would continue, indefinitely, into the future. On June 26, 2000, President Clinton announced that, over the next decade, the federal budget surplus would total nearly $1.9 trillion. This outrageous, deliberate lie to the American people was, in my opinion, the greatest sin of the Clinton presidency. It dwarfed the alleged misconduct that ultimately led to his impeachment.

From that point on, the American people seemed to believe that there truly was excess money in the federal budget, and cunning politicians began building schemes to further mislead the people into believing that surplus money was available for new programs and/or for cutting taxes. Clinton had given birth to a monster, in the form of the budget-surplus myth, which would later enable George W. Bush to get by with reckless actions that would threaten America's economic and budgetary future and contribute immensely to the current economic crises.

How could the President of the United States make such reckless claims? How could the American people be so gullible? The $1.9 trillion projected ten-year surplus that Clinton announced on June 26 was more than 2 ½ times what the administration had predicted it would be just three months earlier in February! How could anybody give any credibility to a projection procedure that yielded a projection that was 2 ½ times as high as it had predicted just three months earlier?

Clinton did signal the dubious nature of this projection by raising the following red flag:

"This is just a budget projection. It would not be prudent to commit every penny of a future surplus that is just a projection and therefore subject to change."

"It would be a big mistake to commit this entire surplus to spending or tax cuts...The projections could be wrong, they could be right."

President Clinton did the country a great disservice with that announcement. He knew how it would be interpreted by the media, and his motives for making the announcement were purely political. After 8 years of dealing with the budget figures, he had to know that the projections were definitely wrong. He also knew that whatever the size of any budget surpluses over the next decade, most, if not all, of it would belong to the Social Security trust fund.

His political motives for making the announcement were twofold. First of all, he wanted to exaggerate just how much the budget picture had improved under his presidency. Secondly, he probably thought the announcement would help Vice President Gore's campaign.

Strangely enough, the announcement probably helped George W. Bush far more than it helped Gore. The cornerstone of Bush's campaign was his proposed large tax cut, and he needed evidence that the cut was affordable. The Bush camp released the following statement in reaction to Clinton's announcement.

> "Today's report confirms the accuracy of the conservative estimates Governor Bush used in preparing his balanced budget plan. The report also demonstrates the importance of passing the governor's tax cuts to prevent all this new money from being spent on bigger government."

The Bush statement just reinforced the belief of many observers that George W. Bush was willing to distort the truth, and deliberately lie to the public in order to get to the White House. How could Governor Bush really believe that there was any new money, except that resulting from the higher Social Security taxes that had been specifically earmarked for funding the retirement of the baby boomers? Surely, Bush was aware that the United States government had more than $4.5 trillion in unpaid bills just from the previous twenty years of deficit spending. The younger Bush should certainly have known that his father's administration had spent $1.1 trillion more than it collected in revenue during President George H.W. Bush's four-year term.

Why wasn't George W. Bush trying to find ways to undo the damage done during the Reagan-Bush years by paying down at least part of the debt accumulated during those years of irresponsible defi-

cit spending? Why would he call for additional tax
cuts if he truly understood the government's financial condition?

Equally irresponsible were the statements of
Vice President Gore. During his acceptance speech
at the Democratic National Convention in Los An-
geles on August 17, 2000, Gore did more than
exaggerate or dream the impossible dream. He
traveled deeply into fantasyland, especially with
regard to his statements about the federal budget.
Below are excerpts from that speech.

> "Not so long ago, a balanced budget seemed
> impossible. Now our budget surpluses make it possible
> to give a full range of targeted tax cuts to working
> families...I'll fight for tax cuts that go to the right
> people...We will balance the budget every year and
> dedicate the budget surplus first to saving Social
> Security. In the next four years, we will pay off all the
> national debt this nation accumulated in our first 200
> years. This will put us on the path to completely
> eliminating the debt by 2012...putting both Social
> Security and Medicare in an iron-clad lockbox where
> the politicians can't touch them. To me, that kind of
> common sense is a family value...Hands off Medicare
> and Social Security trust fund money. I'll veto
> anything that spends it for anything other than Social
> Security and Medicare."

With the benefit of hindsight, readers should be
able to see just how outrageously absurd Gore's
statements were. He was promising tax cuts,
spending increases, a balanced budget every year,
and eliminating the national debt by 2012. The
national debt actually doubled between 2000 and
2009, and it is headed skyward as I write these
words. Of course, as outrageous as Gore's promises

were, they were dwarfed by the promises made by George W. Bush.

As I see it, Bill Clinton, Al Gore, and George W. Bush all ganged up against the American people in 2000 and sold them a bill of goods in the form of the budget-surplus myth. In that sense, they all bear some of the responsibility for the catastrophic events that the world now faces.

Bush gets most of the blame since he is the one who became president and implemented the policies that played a key role in the financial meltdown and economic collapse. However, President Clinton and Vice President Gore were major participants in misleading the public about the financial condition of the United States Government. Clinton gave birth to the budget surplus myth and both Bush and Gore attempted to ride that myth to the oval office.

Once George W. Bush became President, that budget-surplus myth, created by President Clinton, really came in handy. He used it to the hilt to deceive the American people and lead this nation toward economic catastrophe.

On February 27, 2001, President George W. Bush delivered his first State of The Union address to a joint session of Congress and to the American people. In this speech, he laid the foundation for his plan to enact massive tax cuts that would benefit primarily the wealthiest five percent of Americans. He also skillfully pulled the wool over the eyes of the public through a series of deceptive statements designed to convince Congress and the public that the coffers of the United States government were overflowing with billions of surplus dollars for as far as the eye could see. To put it mildly, he deliberately misled the public. To put it more bluntly, he told a very **BIG LIE** to the American people about the financial status of the federal budget. Excerpts from the speech are reproduced below.

"Our new governing vision says government should be active, but limited; engaged, but not overbearing. And my budget is based on that philosophy. It is reasonable, and it is responsible. ...My plan pays down an unprecedented amount of our national debt. And then, when money is still left over, my plan returns it to the people who earned it in the first place.

...To make sure the retirement savings of America's seniors are not diverted in any other program, my budget protects all $2.6 trillion of the Social Security surplus for Social Security, and for Social Security alone.

...My budget has funded a responsible increase in our ongoing operations. It has funded our nation's important priorities, it has protected Social Security and Medicare. And our surpluses are big enough that there is still money left over.

"Many of you have talked about the need to pay down our national debt. I listened and I agree. We owe it to our children and grandchildren to act now, and I hope you will join me to pay down $2 trillion in debt during the next 10 years...That is more debt, repaid more quickly than has ever been repaid by any nation at any time in history.

We should also prepare for the unexpected, for the uncertainties of the future. We should approach our nation's budget as any prudent family would, with a contingency fund for emergencies or additional spending needs. For example, after a strategic review, we may need to increase defense spending. We may need to increase spending for our farmers or additional money to reform Medicare. And so, my budget sets aside almost a trillion dollars over 10 years for additional needs. That is one trillion additional reasons you can feel comfortable supporting this budget.

We have increased our budget at a responsible 4 percent. We have funded our priorities. We paid down all the available debt. We have prepared for contingencies. And we still have money left over.

...Now we come to a fork in the road; we have two choices. ...We could spend the money on more and bigger government. That's the road our nation has traveled in recent years.

...If you continue on that road, you will spend the surplus and have to dip into Social Security to pay other bills. Unrestrained government spending is a dangerous road to deficits, so we must take a different path. The other choice is to let the American people spend their own money to meet their own needs.

I hope you will join me in standing firmly on the side of the people. You see, the growing surplus exists because taxes are too high and government is charging more that it needs. The people of America have been overcharged and, on their behalf, I am here asking for a refund."

Perhaps never before in history had the American people been played for such fools by their president. Most people know very little about such things as economics and the federal budget, and so they must trust someone else to tell them the truth. Surely they could believe a new President, who was asking for their support, to be straightforward with them. If he said the government had trillions of dollars of surplus money, it must be true, regardless of how implausible it seemed. And he wasn't the only top official to say so. Both President Clinton and Vice-president Gore had spoken of large surpluses. At the time of President George W. Bush's 2001 State of the Union address, the United States government owed approximately $5 trillion more than it had owed just twenty years before when President Reagan had taken office. This represented $5 trillion of unpaid bills. Bush's own father had contributed greatly to this massive red-ink spending. During George H. W. Bush's four years as president, the on-budget deficit (excluding Social Security funds) averaged more than $286 billion per year. And, when he left office, the national debt, that had been only $1 trillion at the beginning of the Reagan-Bush administration, had soared above the $4 trillion mark.

President Clinton also ran on-budget deficits during the first six years of his presidency. However, because of the Clinton deficit-reduction package, the deficits declined significantly during each of Clinton's first six years. Finally, in 1999, the deficit was totally eliminated, and there was a surplus of $1.9 billion. In fiscal 2000, the federal budget had a surplus of $86.4 billion. These were the only two non-Social Security surpluses during the preceding 40-year period, and they will probably be the only two surpluses that most Americans will see during their entire lifetimes.

George W. Bush should have been in a better position than almost anyone else to know just how dire the federal budget situation was, and what a dismal failure Reaganomics had been during the 12 years of Reagan and Bush. His father was vice president for 8 years under Reagan, and served four years as president. As the son of the vice president for eight years, and as the son of the President of the United States for 4 years, George W. Bush had access to information not available to most people.

With aspirations to be President, himself, someday, the younger Bush must have talked shop with his father and tried to learn as much about the job as possible. Certainly he had to know that during those 12 years of Reagan and Bush, the national debt had quadrupled. Didn't he have any concern that Ronald Reagan and the elder Bush had added three times as much to the national debt in just 12 years as all the previous presidents in American history had added in nearly 200 years?

He must have shared his father's pain when the elder Bush failed to win reelection. And all he had to do to learn why his father had been defeated was to read the news. It was the economy and the massive deficits that did his father in, and it was Clinton's promise to reduce the deficits that brought victory to him. Knowing about those massive deficits during the Reagan-Bush years, and knowing how much the national debt had risen in just a few years, how could George W. Bush keep a straight face when he told the American people that the government had surplus money?

There was no surplus money, except for the Social Security fund, and Bush pledged not to touch that money. As for the surpluses in 1999 and 2000, during the Clinton administration, they weren't large enough to even offset the 1997 deficit of $103.4 billion, let alone the other Clinton deficits. The surpluses of 1999 and 2000 came at the peak of the business cycle when the economy was in overdrive, and the unemployment rate was at a 30-year low. Only under such conditions did the economy have the potential to generate enough revenue to even balance the budget. And let's remember that those two years were preceded by 38 consecutive years of deficits.

So where did President Bush think there was going to be surplus revenue? The surpluses in the Social Security fund, that would last only a few more years before turning into deficits, were specifically earmarked for payment of the increased benefits that would coincide with the retirement of the baby boomers. And, once again, Bush had pledged that the Social Security surpluses would not be used for anything but the payment of Social Security benefits.

There was no way that there could be ongoing surpluses in the non-Social Security budget, as Bush learned when he ran a budget deficit during his very first year in office. The tax structure was barely capable of generating enough revenue to balance the budget in the top phase of the business cycle when all resources were employed and the economy was producing at its maximum capacity. Only rarely, and for short periods of time, is the economy at this stage. At all other times, the economy is either in recession or in the process of recovering from the last recession. During such times, the economy is not operating at the full-employment level, and experience over the previous 40 years had shown that in most years there would be at least a small deficit.

Despite these facts, President Bush told the nation that the government had massive surpluses. He does not use qualifying words such as "projected surplus" or "anticipated surplus." He talked of the surplus as if he already had it locked in a vault. Consider the following statement:

> "We have increased our budget at a responsible 4 percent. We have funded our priorities. We paid down all the available debt. We have prepared for contingencies. And we still have money left over."

George W. Bush was talking about make-believe money, but he led his audience to believe that it was the real thing. He and his staff had concocted a make-believe, fantasy-land budget, and they had manipulated the numbers in such a way as to create make-believe surpluses.

Bush had not yet done any of the things he referred to. Certainly he had not paid down any of the national debt. On the contrary, he would add more than $4 trillion to the national debt during the next eight years. He would break the lock on the Social Security lockbox during his very first year, and, during his second year, he would still not have enough money to pay the bills after spending all of the Social Security money. And there would never be any money left over, not even play money. He explained the reason for the nonexistent surplus as follows:

> "The growing surplus exists because taxes are too high and government is charging more than it needs. The people of America have been overcharged and, on their behalf, I am here asking for a refund."

There was no growing surplus, except for the temporary, planned surplus in the Social Security fund. The non-Social Security budget had run deficits in 38 of the past 40 years. How could he say that the government was charging more in taxes than it needed when his own father had run an average non-Social Security deficit of more than $286 billion per year during his four years as President, and President Clinton had run deficits during 6 of his 8 years as President?

President George W. Bush, who was asking for the trust and support of the American people, deliberately deceived them during his very first State of the Union address. He did so in order to pass a massive tax cut that he knew was not in the best interest of the nation or the economy. It was political payback time. Those wealthy supporters who had given so much money to Bush's campaign had to be repaid. Otherwise, they might not be so generous when he ran for a second term.

Despite Bush's continuing claims that there was plenty of non-Social Security surplus to fund his tax cuts, and despite his pledge not to use any of the Social Security surplus for anything but Social Security, when the numbers were in for fiscal 2001, the government ran a $33.4 billion deficit. The surplus of $86.4 billion during the last year of the Clinton presidency would be the last surplus for a very long time, if not forever.

The terrorist attacks of September 11, 2001, and the two wars that followed, greatly worsened the financial status of the federal government. However, the budget was already in deficit territory even before the terrorist attacks. There has been a tendency for some to attribute the financial problems to the increased military spending and let Bush off the hook for his financial mismanagement. However, the budget problems are a reflection of both the increased military spending and the reckless and irresponsible fiscal policy of the Bush administration.

The first year's record of Bush's economic and budgetary policies is very significant, because it was not in any way related to the terrorist attacks or the resulting wars against terrorism and Iraq. Fiscal year 2001 ended on September 30, just 19 days after the September 11 attacks, so there was not enough time for any effects to be reflected in that year's budget. The first of the expenditures on war would not show up until the 2002 budget year. Therefore, Bush was fully responsible for the fiscal 2001 deficit.

The Social Security Lockbox was broken into during Bush's very first year in office. I think there is little doubt that Bush knew he would be dipping into Social Security before the end of his term, but even he was probably surprised that the need came so soon. It had been only four months since the $1.35 trillion, ten-year, tax cut had been enacted into law. Bush had assured the nation at that time that huge budget surpluses lay ahead as far as the eye could see. Yet, four months later, the government was forced to dip into the Social Security trust fund in order to pay its bills. Because of the unaffordable tax cuts, the government was in deep financial trouble months before that terrible day in September.

CHAPTER THREE

The Social Security Trust Fund

On February 25, 2004, in testimony before the House Budget Committee, Federal Reserve Chairman, Alan Greenspan, launched a verbal bombshell which set off a political storm throughout the nation by proposing cutting future Social Security benefits. Social Security had not received much public attention since it had allegedly been fixed by the Social Security Amendments of 1983, and most Americans believed that the program was fiscally sound. Thus, Greenspan's call for trimming benefits for future retirees touched a nerve in many Americans, especially those nearing retirement.

Greenspan said, "We are over-committed at this stage. It is important that we tell people who are about to retire what it is they will have." He warned that the government should not "promise more than we are able to deliver." Pointing to the forthcoming retirement of the baby-boom generation as the reason for his concern, Greenspan said, "This dramatic demographic change is certain to place enormous demands on our nation's resources—demands we will almost surely be unable to meet unless action is taken. For a variety of reasons, that action is better taken as soon as possible."

Six months later, on August 27, 2004, Greenspan again spoke of cutting Social Security benefits during remarks at a symposium in Jackson Hole, Wyoming. "As a nation, we owe it to our retirees to promise only the benefits that can be delivered," Greenspan said. "If we have promised more than our economy has the ability to deliver to retirees without unduly diminishing real income gains of workers, as I fear we may have, we must recalibrate our public programs so that pending retirees have time to adjust through other channels."

Like his February statement, this new statement on Social Security by the Fed Chairman generated a lot of news coverage, and the idea that Social Security might be in some kind of long-term financial trouble began to take root in the minds of at least some Americans. Greenspan's comments, along with the propaganda that had long been spread by conservative think tanks, served as seeds of doubt as to whether or not Social Security was really as solvent as most people thought. These early statements laid the foundation for President George W. Bush's then secret plan to launch an assault against the Social Security program once he was safely re-elected to a second term.

Federal Reserve Chairman, Alan Greenspan, knew better than anyone just how solvent Social Security actually was, or at least should be. The 1983 payroll tax increase, enacted upon the recommendation of the National Commission on Social Security, headed by Greenspan, had allegedly "fixed" the baby boomer problem with regard to

Social Security. That law required the baby boomers to pay enough taxes to fund the benefits of current retirees, plus enough additional taxes to prepay most of the cost of their own Social Security benefits. The additional tax revenue was supposed to be saved and put into the Social Security Trust Fund to build up a large reserve earmarked specifically for the retirement of the baby boomers. This reserve would be used to supplement the payroll tax revenue so that full benefits could be paid throughout the period of the boomers' retirement years without placing a disproportionate burden on the younger generation.

The 1983 legislation marked a sharp break with the traditional pay-as-you-go approach to funding Social Security benefits. After 1983, the Social Security system no longer operated on a strictly pay-as-you-go basis. For the baby-boom generation, Social Security has operated on a combination "pay-as-you-go" and "prepay-your-own-benefits" principle. By the time the baby boomers retire, they will have prepaid a major portion of the entire cost of their benefits, as well as having funded the retirement benefits of retirees during the years between 1983 and their own retirement.

What Greenspan and Bush were attempting to do was to distract public attention away from the real Social Security culprit—the fact that the government had "borrowed" every cent of the surplus Social Security money generated by the 1983 payroll tax increase and used it to finance tax cuts and other government spending programs. If the government had saved and invested the surplus revenue, we would not be facing any short-term Social-Security funding problem today. There would be enough money to pay full benefits until the year 2041.

Payroll tax revenue, which has been greatly exceeding benefit payments ever since the 1983 Social Security tax increase, will cross the line in 2017 and, thereafter, it will be inadequate to fund full benefit payments. This was foreseen and provided for in the plan recommended by the Greenspan Commission report of 1982. The government increased payroll taxes in 1983 by enough to generate surpluses for all years up to 2017. If the Social Security surplus revenue had been saved and invested, as was the intent of the 1983 law, the trust fund would hold approximately $3.7 trillion in real assets by 2017 when the surpluses will come to an end.

Unfortunately, over the years, both Republicans and Democrats have spent the money, that was supposed to be going into the Social Security reserve, on other things. Because of the looting of the surplus money, the government will be unable to pay full Social Security benefits after 2017 without a tax increase. Most Americans seem to believe that their Social Security contributions go into a special trust fund where it accumulates, and then, when they retire, the money will be paid back to them out of the trust fund. The notion that the government has spent all those Social Security contributions that weren't needed to pay current benefits, to fund Bush's income tax cuts and for other government programs, is unthinkable to most Americans. They cannot believe our government would take revenue that was collected specifically for Social Security and spend it on other programs.

This would be like using Grandma's retirement fund to pay current expenses because Grandma won't need the money until she actually retires. Any individual, who would drain the retirement fund of his or her grandmother, without telling her, and without making any provisions for repayment of the funds when Grandma reached retirement age and needed the money, would be branded a scoundrel and a criminal. Yet, that is exactly what the United States Government has been doing with the Social Security surplus revenue since 1985.

The revenue from the Social Security payroll tax, earmarked exclusively for the payment of Social Security benefits, is routinely deposited into the general fund and all money, that is not needed to pay current benefits, is spent as if it were general revenue. This is fraudulent, and it is a violation of Section 13301 of the Budget Enforcement Act of 1990, which explicitly prohibits co-mingling Social Security funds with general revenue funds. There had never been any significant Social Security surplus prior to the 1983 tax increase. On the contrary, Social Security ran small deficits for seven years in a row from 1976 to 1982. However, that changed with enactment of the 1983 tax increase.

The problem is that there is not a penny in the trust fund. The government of the United States has raided the trust fund on a regular basis for more than two decades and spent the surplus money on other government programs. Presidents Ronald Reagan, George H.W. Bush, Bill Clinton and George W. Bush have all been participants in this ongoing fraud against the American people. Even as President Bush traveled around the country, during his privatization campaign, claiming that he wanted to "save" and "strengthen" Social Security, he continued to bleed the program to death.

The events of the past 25 years have led many Americans to question the commitment of current politicians to keeping the fund solvent for future generations. The Social Security program has become a source of political maneuvering and a mask for irresponsible fiscal policies.

The 1983 legislation was designed specifically for the purpose of building up a surplus in the trust fund in preparation for the retirement of the baby boomers. Both Social Security tax rates and the Social Security tax base were gradually raised over a seven-year period so the trust fund would be solvent when it took the big financial hit resulting from the retirement of the baby boomers, the largest generation in American history.

Unfortunately, instead of using the increased Social Security revenue to build up the size of the trust fund for future retirees as was intended, the government began using the surplus to fund other government programs as soon as it first appeared in 1985, and has continued to do so ever since. This practice has masked the true size of federal budget deficits because each year since 1985 the government subtracted the surplus in the Social Security trust fund from the deficit in the operating budget and reported an official budget deficit that was billions of dollars below the actual deficit.

Table 3-1 shows the actual size of the Social Security surplus for every year from 1985 to 2008, and the cumulative totals of Social Security dollars borrowed by the government and used for non-Social

Security purposes for each year in the period. Prior to 1983, the Social Security fund ran deficits for seven consecutive years.   There was a deficit of $7.9 billion in 1982, the last year before enactment of the 1983 tax increases.

Both 1983 and 1984 were essentially break-even years. However, the revenue generating capacity of the 1983 tax hikes becomes clear for 1985 and the years that follow. The $9.4 billion Social Security surplus of 1985 had increased tenfold by 1998, with a surplus of $99.2 billion recorded for that year.

Although the Social Security fund has been running surpluses for several years because of the 1983 tax increases, beginning in 2017, the annual benefits payments are expected to exceed the annual revenue, and the Social Security deficit will widen with each passing year after that.

The Social Security Amendments of 1983 laid the foundation for the worst fiscal fraud in the nation's history. The new legislation generated a Social Security surplus of $9.4 billion in 1985 with increasingly larger yearly surpluses thereafter. The Social Security surplus was $38.8 billion in 1988, $56.6 billion in 1990, and $99.2 billion in 1998.

The Social Security trust fund ran surpluses totaling $211.7 billion during President George H.W. Bush's four-year term, and Bush spent every dollar of the surplus funds on other government programs. He ran average annual on-budget deficits of more than $286 billion per year, and the national debt, that had been only $1 trillion at the beginning of the Reagan-Bush administration, had soared above the $4 trillion mark by the time Bush left office.

TABLE 3-1
SOCIAL SECURITY SURPLUS 1985-2008
IN BILLIONS OF DOLLARS

Year	Social Security Surplus for the Year	Cumulative Social Security Surpluses, 1985 and After	Cumulative Social Security Funds Borrowed and Spent for Non-Social Security Purposes, 1985 and After
1985	+9.2	9.2	9.2
1986	+16.7	25.9	25.9
1987	+18.6	44.5	44.5
1988	+37.1	81.6	81.6
1989	+52.8	134.4	134.4
1990	+56.6	191.0	191.0
1991	+52.2	243.2	243.2
1992	+50.1	293.3	293.3
1993	+45.3	338.6	338.6
1994	+55.7	394.3	394.3
1995	+62.4	456.7	456.7
1996	+66.6	523.3	523.3
1997	+81.4	604.7	604.7
1998	+99.2	703.9	703.9
1999	+123.7	827.6	827.6
2000	+149.8	977.4	977.4
2001	+160.7	1,138.1	1,138.1
2002	+159.7	1,297.8	1,297.8
2003	+160.8	1,458.6	1,458.6
2004	+155.2	1,613.8	1,613.8
2005	+175.3	1,789.1	1,789.1
2006	+186.3	1,975.4	1,975.4
2007	+181.5	2,156.9	2,156.9
2008*	+192.2	2,349.1	2,349.1

*Estimate

Source: Economic Report of the President, 2008

Earlier presidents did not have an opportunity to deceive the American people in this way. Even during the first four years of the Reagan administration, the Social Security system ran a net deficit of $12.4 billion. It was only during the second Reagan term, and after, that the planned Social Security surpluses, resulting from the Social Security Amendments of 1983, made possible the fraudulent misappropriation of federal funds by elected officials.

George W. Bush, Bill Clinton, Bush's father, and Ronald Reagan spent every dollar of the Social Security surplus resulting from the 1983 Social Security tax increase. All of that money will eventually be needed to pay Social Security benefits. However, it has already been spent on other government programs.

The Social Security Trust Fund was supposed to be kept separate from the general operating budget from the very beginning, but it was not until passage of the Budget Enforcement Act of 1990 that there was an actual federal law prohibiting comingling the two funds.

Senator Ernest Hollings (D-SC) was outraged by the fraudulent Social Security practices, and he sought to make them illegal. Hollings' proposal eventually became Section 13301 of the Budget Enforcement Act of 1990, which was signed into law by President George H. W. Bush on November 5, 1990. It prohibited including Social Security funds in any budget calculations including deficits or surpluses.

Section 13301 explicitly states:

Not withstanding any other provision of law, the receipts and disbursements of the Federal Old Age and Survivors Insurance Trust Fund and the Federal Disability Insurance Trust Fund shall not be counted as new budget authority, outlays, receipts, or deficit or surplus for purposes of (1) the budget of the United States Government as submitted by the President, (2) the Congressional budget, or (3) the Balanced Budget and Emergency Deficit Control Act of 1985.

Senator Hollings thought that, by making it illegal for the Congress and the President to include Social Security funds in their budget calculations, the deliberate deception of the public would come to an end. But he was wrong. The Bush administration and members of Congress got over this tiny hurdle by simply ignoring the law. They continued their deceptive practices just as they had done before. But there was a difference. Now they were guilty of more than deception. Now they were guilty of deliberately violating federal law.

Table 3-2 shows the non-Social Security surplus or deficit, and the Social Security surplus or deficit, from 1981 through 2008, as well as the public debt at the end of each fiscal year. Prior to 1983, Social Security had operated on a pay-as-you-go basis with no large surpluses. This practice worked fine so long as the number of new retirees each year remained relatively stable. However, the Presidential Commission headed by Alan Greenspan noted in 1982 that a major problem would develop when the baby-boom generation began retiring in about 2010.

There would be such an acceleration in the number of retirees over a period of several years that the trust fund could not possibly remain solvent without massive amounts of new revenue. It should be remembered that these annual surpluses were a part of the blueprint designed to get the fund ready for the baby boomers and that the fund will again begin to experience annual deficits in about 2017. This money from the temporary surplus years was to be set aside for the specific purpose of keeping the Social Security fund solvent when it took the big financial hit resulting from the retirement of the baby boomers. Instead, government leaders defied the intent of the 1983 legislation and used the surplus dollars to pay for other government programs, and ultimately to help finance major tax cuts.

The government deliberately deceived the public into believing that the planned Social Security surplus was really a general revenue surplus, and President George W. Bush used this fraud-based public perception to justify enactment of his massive $1.35 trillion tax cut. As things turned out, this tax cut for the rich was paid for primarily with funds generated by the regressive Social Security payroll tax levied on American workers.

Social Security taxes, like all other Government revenues, are deposited in the U.S. Treasury and become part of the Government's operating cash pool. Through separate accounting entries, the government keeps a record of how much money is supposed to be in the Social Security trust fund. Similarly, Social Security benefits are paid from the Treasury, not from the trust fund. Essentially, the only way that Social Security receipts and payments are kept separate from other government financing, is through bookkeeping entries.

TABLE: 3-2
NON-SOCIAL SECURITY SURPLUSES OR DEFICTS,
SOCIAL SECURITY SURPLUSES OR DEFICITS, AND
PUBLIC DEBT 1981-2008, IN BILLIONS OF DOLLARS

Year	Non-Social Security Surplus(+) or Deficit(-)	Social Security Surplus(+) or Deficit(-)	Public Debt End of Fiscal Year
1981	-73.9	-5.1	994.8
1982	-120.6	-7.4	1,137.3
1983	-207.7	-.1	1,371.7
1984	-185.3	-.1	1,564.6
1985	-221.5	+9.2	1,817.4
1986	-237.9	+16.7	2,120.5
1987	-168.4	+18.6	2,346.0
1988	-192.3	+37.1	2,601.1
1989	-205.4	+52.8	2,867.8
1990	-277.6	+56.6	3,206.3
1991	-321.4	+52.2	3,598.2
1992	-340.4	+50.1	4,001.8
1993	-300.4	+45.3	4,351.0
1994	-258.8	+55.7	4,643.3
1995	-226.4	+62.4	4,920.6
1996	-174.0	+66.6	5,181.5
1997	-103.2	+81.4	5,369.2
1998	-29.9	+99.2	5,478.2
1999	+1.9	+123.7	5,605.5
2000	+86.4	+149.8	5,628.7
2001	-32.4	+160.7	5,769.9
2002	-317.4	+159.7	6,198.4
2003	-538.4	+160.8	6,760.0
2004	-568.0	+155.2	7,354.7
2005	-493.6	175.3	7,905.3
2006	-434.5	+186.3	8,451.4
2007	-343.5	+181.5	8,950.7
2008*	-602.2	+192.2	9,654.4

*Estimates
Source: Economic Report of the President, 2008

Government IOUs called "special issues of the Treasury" are posted to the account of the Social Security trust fund. These "special-issue" securities have no commercial value because they cannot be sold in the marketplace. These IOUs represent a promise by the government that it will obtain resources in the future equal to the value of the securities whenever such resources are needed to pay Social Security benefits. However, in order to do so, the government would have to raise taxes, cut spending, or borrow the money from the public.

These IOUs are supposed to be earning interest, but the government pays the interest on funds borrowed from the Social Security trust fund with nonmarketable "special-issue" securities just like the ones posted when the money was borrowed. This means that both the assets and the earnings of the Social Security trust fund are in the form of government IOUs that have no commercial value.

Despite the claims to the contrary by various groups and individuals, the Social Security trust fund contains no real assets. All the surplus revenue generated by the payroll tax increase of 1983 has been spent by the government on other programs. Therefore, when the revenue from the payroll tax falls below the cost of Social Security benefits, beginning in 2017, the government will be unable to pay full benefits from the payroll tax alone.

The main source of confusion with regard to whether or not the trust fund holds real assets is the accounting trickery that is used by the government to make it look like the trust fund holds real assets despite the fact that it does not. Most people don't understand that public issue marketable Treasury bonds are something very different from the non-marketable special issue government IOUs that are held by the Social Security trust fund. By law, any Social Security surplus is supposed to be invested in financial instruments "backed by the full faith and credit of the United States Government." This means that Social Security funds cannot be invested in stocks, commercial bonds, real estate, or even FDIC insured bank accounts.

The Treasury has only two options that meet the letter of the law. The first option is to invest the Social Security surplus in public issue marketable Treasury bonds purchased in the open market from the public. These are the type of United States Treasury bonds held by Japanese pension funds, the Chinese government, Bill Gates, and every other private investor who owns marketable United States Treasury bonds.

Let's look at an example of how this would work. Suppose that Bill Gates decides to sell $10 million of his U. S. Treasury bond holdings in the open market in order to raise capital for expansion. Now suppose that the Social Security trustees use $10 million of Social Security surplus to buy public issue marketable Treasury bonds in the open market and, just by chance, end up with the bonds that Bill Gates sold. The net effect is that 10 million surplus Social Security dollars end up in the hands of Bill Gates, and the Social Security trust fund ends up with $10 million of good-as-gold marketable Treasury bonds that it can resell in the open market any time it needs to raise money with which to pay benefits. None of the $10 million is available for the President and Congress to spend because it is all saved and truly invested in real assets. It earns real interest, and the Treasury bonds can be resold in the open market at any time.

Now let's look at what really happens to that $10 million, and every other dollar of Social Security surplus revenue that is supposed to be in the trust fund. The government takes the money and spends it just as if it were general fund revenue. How has the government gotten by with this for all these years? It has done so by creating a special type of government document that meets the letter of the law, but not the spirit. When the government spends Social Security money, it replaces the money with pieces of paper called special issue bonds. These so-called "bonds" have printed on their face, "Backed by the full faith and credit of the United States government." This fulfills the legal requirement that Social Security funds be held only in the form of instruments backed by the full faith and credit of the government. However, it does not meet the spirit of the law.

These special issue IOUs are available to, and held by, only the government trust funds. They are not marketable and therefore cannot be bought or sold at any price. They are not real assets, and they have no market value. The special issue IOU's cannot be used to raise funds for Social Security benefit payments. They serve only as an accounting record of how much Social Security money has been spent by the government on other programs.

Money can be spent, or it can be saved and invested. But once money is spent, there is nothing left to invest. Not a single dollar of the trust fund money has been invested in anything. It was taken and spent, pure and simple. The IOUs in the trust fund are simply an accounting record of how much money the government took.

On the official Social Security website (http://www.socialsecurity.gov/qa.htm), there is the following statement: *"Money not needed to pay to-day's benefits is invested in special-issue Treasury bonds."* This statement is not true. The surplus money is "loaned" to the government who spends it on other programs. None of the Social Security money is invested in anything.

David Walker, the Comptroller General of the United States Government Accountability Office (GAO), confirmed this fact On January 21, 2005, when he said,

> "The left hand owes the right hand, and that has legal, political and moral significance. But it doesn't have any economic significance whatsoever. There are no stocks or bonds or real estate in the trust fund. It has nothing of real value to draw down."

The key words are *"special-issue* Treasury bonds." These are not real bonds like everyone else invests in. They are a gimmick created by the government to abide by the letter of the law that Social Security funds must be invested in government securities, but they are not consistent with the spirit of the law. They are simply accounting records of the money the government has "borrowed" from the fund and spent on other programs. They are simply IOUs which have no value unless the government finds a way to pay the money back.

We can say that the government just borrowed the money, but the word "borrow" implies repayment. The government has been taking and spending this money ever since the first surpluses began to show up in 1985, and absolutely no provisions have been made for repayment of any of it. The government has neither enacted future tax increases that are scheduled to kick in when the money needs to be repaid, nor has it targeted any specific government spending programs that are scheduled to be eliminated whenever repayment of the "borrowed" Social Security money becomes necessary. Unless and until provisions have been made for repaying the "borrowed" money, I think it is more appropriate to think of the money as stolen.

Suppose it is discovered that a bank employee has been taking money from the bank for 23 years, and altering the books to cover up his actions. If the employee insists that he just "borrowed" the money and plans to repay it in some way at some unknown time in the future, will the employee be allowed to continue the practice and avoid punishment because he is only "borrowing" the money. Absolutely not! Once discovered, the "borrowing" will be immediately stopped and the employee will be arrested and charged with embezzlement because he took money that did not belong to him and spent it as if it were his own.

Isn't this what the federal government has been doing? Hasn't it taken money that was collected specifically for the Social Security program and spent it on programs for which the money was not intended? Indeed it has. The federal government has used fraudulent accounting practices to divert

the money from Social Security into other programs
without the public's knowledge or consent. The
government has embezzled every dollar of the
Social Security surplus revenue generated by the
1983 Social Security Amendments, and it continues
to embezzle more than $500 million of Social
Security money each and every day.

Will the government repay the Social Security
money that it has spent, and thus enable Social
Security to pay full benefits until 2041 as planned?
Some people react to this question as if it is not
even worthy of an answer. "Of course the
government will repay the money," they say. "The
United State government always pays its debts."

But it is not quite that cut and dried. The
financial outlook for the federal budget is the
bleakest it has ever been. The government has
increased the national debt from $1 trillion in 1981
to more than $11 trillion today, and the debt
continues to skyrocket at an alarming rate.
Furthermore, the public has been conditioned for
the past quarter century to think of tax increases as
just about the worst of all conceivable sins.

Americans have never liked paying taxes, but at
least they reluctantly supported enough taxation to
meet the nation's needs prior to the Reagan
presidency. However, Reagan convinced the people
that they were being overtaxed, and he pushed
through huge tax cuts that gave birth to years of
record deficits and a skyrocketing national debt.
President Clinton's deficit-reduction package
squeaked through the Congress without a single
Republican vote, and the tax increase portion of the

package was portrayed by many as just about the most evil thing any president could possibly do.

Under Clinton, the deficits became smaller and smaller during the first six years, and there were modest surpluses in 1999 and 2000—the first surpluses in 38 years. However, George W. Bush once again convinced the American people that they were being overtaxed.

In his first State of the Union address, delivered on February 27, 2001, Bush laid the foundation for his plan to enact massive tax cuts, that would benefit primarily the wealthiest five percent of Americans, and be funded primarily with Social Security surplus revenue. He skillfully misled the public through a series of deceptive statements designed to convince Congress that the coffers of the United States government were overflowing with billions of surplus dollars for as far as the eye could see. "Deceptive statements" is putting it mildly. To put it more bluntly, he lied to the American people about the financial status of the federal budget.

The next two chapters will provide an analysis of government economic policies under Presidents Bill Clinton and George W. Bush. Chapter 4 will trace the economic progress that accompanied the return to traditional economic policies during the Clinton years. As a result of his deficit-reduction program, Clinton managed to eliminate the deficits and have surpluses in 1999 and 2000.

In Chapter 5, we will see how George W. Bush gave us a new round of Reaganomics. He pushed through Congress two major tax cuts which resulted in a return to large deficits and a skyrocketing national debt.

CHAPTER FOUR

The Clinton Years

The likelihood that a little-known governor from Arkansas would be elected President in 1992 seemed almost nonexistent as little as a year before the election. President George H. W. Bush was riding so high in the polls that most of the leading potential Democratic challengers chose not to even enter the race. Bush had been the Commander-In-Chief in the Gulf War, the most decisive American Military Victory since World War II, and most observers believed that Bush would be unbeatable in 1992.

After a stormy primary campaign, among a field of what most political experts considered "lightweight" candidates, Bill Clinton, the then governor of Arkansas, was nominated as the 1992 Democratic candidate. However, most observers still thought the nomination was not worth having and expected Clinton to serve as the sacrificial lamb for the Democrat party. Some of the losing candidates, and those would-be candidates who had chosen not to run, tended to just write off the 1992 election as a lost cause and set their sights on 1996.

Bill Clinton, however, never saw himself as a sacrificial lamb, and he was determined to become the next President of the United States. The boy from Hope, Arkansas, who had once considered becoming a professional saxophone player, had set his sights on the White House while still in high school. As a delegate to Boys Nation, Clinton met President John F. Kennedy in the White House Rose Garden, and the encounter changed his life forever. He decided to enter a life of politics and public service, and he expected to someday return to the White House as President.

Despite his popularity as a wartime president, Bush soon discovered just how important the economy was to American voters. Ross Perot, a self-made billionaire, entered the race as a third-party candidate and ran a one-issue campaign on deficit reduction. Clinton hit hard on the deficit, but also emphasized the need for a major change in Washington. He convinced enough voters, who were looking for change, to vote for him that he received 43.3 percent of the popular vote, compared to 37.7 percent for Bush, and 19 percent for Perot. In terms of the electoral votes, the race wasn't even close. Clinton got 370 votes compared to Bush's 168.

Clinton had promised to reduce the deficit, and he was determined to do so, no matter how unpopular his prescription was with the established Washington politicians. He proposed a deficit reduction plan that included both major spending cuts and higher taxes. There was immediate stiff opposition to the plan because it included higher taxes. The Republican party had benefited immensely from the credit it got from the Reagan tax cuts, despite the fact that the Reagan cuts were the primary cause of the ongoing massive budget deficits. The Congressional Republicans were determined to block any effort to raise taxes.

The Republican doomsayers argued that passage of the Clinton economic plan would wreck the economy. House Minority Leader Robert H. Michel (R-IL), portrayed Clinton as a traditional tax-and-spend Democrat who was trying to obscure that truth with "the biggest propaganda campaign in recent political history." One House Republican said the Clinton budget was a "recipe for economic and fiscal disaster," and another one said the package "would put the economy in the gutter."

Congressman Dana Rohrabacher (R-CA) rose on the House Floor and said, "Mr. Speaker, I rise in strong opposition to the Clinton tax increase, the largest tax increase in American history, which will hit the middle class, bring our economy to a standstill and in the end increase the deficit."

Republican Congressman Christopher Cox, also from California, was even more graphic in denouncing the Clinton plan. He said, "This is really the Dr. Kevorkian plan for our economy. It will kill jobs, kill businesses, and yes, kill even the higher tax revenues that these suicidal tax increasers hope to gain."

Senate Republicans were equally harsh in their denouncement of the Clinton economic plan. Senator Robert Dole said, "As the President and congressional Democrats busily work on the biggest tax increase in the history of the world, the American people are watching, and they do not like what they see. To put it simply, the Clinton tax increase promises to turn the American dream into a nightmare for millions of hardworking Americans."

One of the most emotionally charged debates on the Clinton economic plan took place on the floor of the Senate on April 3, 1993 between Senator Christopher Bond (R-MO) and Senator Robert Byrd (D-WV). The differences in the two senators' assessment of the effects of the economic and fiscal policies during the previous 12 years of Republican rule, and their projections as to how the Clinton economic plan would affect the economy and the budget in the years ahead were like night and day. Excerpts from the Senators' remarks are reproduced from the Congressional Record below.

"Mr. Bond. Mr. President, this debate is about keeping faith with the American people. This debate is about ensuring that the Federal Government does not destroy our economy. We have heard today that the stock market took a heavy hit yesterday and was down, and that consumer confidence is down.

I think I can tell you the reason that confidence is down. I think I can tell you why the markets are saying we are not going to see profits, we are not going to see growth, we are not going to see jobs, because this body—appropriately enough on April Fools' Day—passed a budget resolution saying that we would increase taxes a whopping $273 billion. The tax rates that would be jacked up under that resolution may contend that they will raise $273 billion. But we have learned something about taxes, and that is that taxes discourage economic activity. ...

...If you look at the economic game plan that President Clinton has asked for and that the majority in both Houses have adopted, the economic game plan is a recipe for disaster. This so-called stimulus package, which I think is more appropriately labeled an "emergency deficit increase package," is going in exactly the opposite direction of what is needed. ...

...But with 273 billion dollar's worth of tax increases, the Clinton plan, endorsed by this body, turns back up again and by the year 2000 the deficit is back up to $300 billion a year....

...Our leader, Senator Dole, with our Budget Committee leader, Senator Domenici, presented an alternative budget deficit reduction plan that would save more than the Clinton budget adopted by this body would save, and they did it without increasing taxes. ...

...At some point, the Government is not going to be able to finance its debt. We are essentially going to be bankrupt.

But, in any event, we are going to be putting a tremendous burden on our children and our children's children. They are going to have to pay taxes on that. They are not going to enjoy the standard of living we have, or certainly the standard of living we would like to see them have, because our increased taxes in the budget resolution—the increases in spending there, plus the increased spending that is proposed in this package before us—will go on to their credit cards. And that is a dirty trick.

I see many young people coming to Washington, full of hope, full of optimism. I am embarrassed to tell them that we have already put $4 trillion of debt on their credit cards.

And during the first—and I trust the only—Clinton administration, we would add another $1.25 trillion to that debt.

The Republican members of this body are united. We have fought to bring some economic sense out of our current budget. We have said: "Cut the additional spending. Don't jack up taxes, particularly when they are going to kill jobs." ...

...We talk about 7 percent unemployment. I believe that the taxes in this measure will drive that unemployment figure even higher, and thus add to the deficit. Spending, if it is left unchecked, is going to drive the deficit back up even with taxes.

We believe the time has come to get serious about the deficit. And the only way to get serious is to cut spending. ...

...The American people are tired of the politics of the past, where Congress continued to vote more and more money without regard to revenues. The tax-and-spend philosophy has not worked. We are attempting to keep faith with the American people who thought we would get a handle on spending.

If we spend money now, and more money that the Government does not have, we will leave the bill for someone else down the road—and that is our children.

Mr. President, there is much more that could be said about this, but I know others want to speak."

Senator Bond painted a very scary picture of what would happen to the American economy and the federal budget if President Clinton's economic package was enacted into law, and he didn't even hint at a link between the Reagan tax cuts and the soaring budget deficits. Senator Byrd, however saw both the past and the future through very different lenses than Senator Bond. Excerpts from Senator Byrd's remarks are reproduced below.

"Mr. Byrd. Mr. President, the distinguished Senator said the time has come to get serious about the deficit.

Mr. President, let us go back over the past 12 years and talk about this deficit that the distinguished Senator has said the time has come to get serious about.

Up until the first fiscal year for which Mr. Reagan was responsible, there had been no triple-digit billion-dollar deficit. Throughout the previous 39 administrations and the previous 192 years of history, this country had never run a triple-digit billion-dollar deficit.

We had gotten into some double-digit billion-dollar deficits under Mr. Ford, $70 billion, $50 billion the next year; under Mr. Carter, $55 billion, $38 billion, $73 billion, and $74 billion.

Then came the Reagan era. The first fiscal year for which Mr. Reagan was responsible, a $120 billion deficit. Never heard of before; unheard of before.

The next year, $208 billion; the next year, $186 billion; the next year, $222 billion; the next year; $238 billion; the next year, $169 billion; the next year, $194 billion; the next year, $250 billion; the next year, $278 billion.

That is the first fiscal year for which Mr. Bush was responsible. He had been trained very well under Mr. Reagan, his predecessor.

So in his first fiscal year for which he was responsible, a $278 billion deficit; the next year, $322 billion; the next year, $340 billion; and the next year, $352 billion.

Now, Mr. President, we hear all of this palavering about the deficit; the time has come to get serous about the deficit.

After all of this?

Our new President is trying to get serious. He has just been in office 73 days. He has sent up a package which is a well-balanced package. It is composed of three elements: deficit reduction, long-term investment in infrastructure, and short-term jobs investment. That is what the bill before the Senate does.

Now, the distinguished Senator from Missouri says, and I am quoting him: "The tax-and-spend philosophy will not work."

Well, Mr. President, what I have just shown about this chart concerning the Federal deficits, fiscal years 1979-93—there are the deficits. We are told now that the tax and spend philosophy will not work. Under the Reagan administration, under the Bush administration, we were following a borrow and spend philosophy, a borrow and spend philosophy.

Mr. President, what happened to the total debt as a result of these deficits? When we run deficits, we increase the debt. We are talking about the last 12 years. We are not talking about the previous 192 years in this

Republic's history, during which time the country ran up a total of $932 billion in debt; $932 billion. Less than $1 trillion. But because of the budgets that occurred during the Reagan and Bush years, the triple-digit billion-dollar deficits, we ran up a debt of $4,114 billion as of March 1, 1993.

So when the distinguished Senator says he is embarrassed when school children ask him, why do we not do something? What is happening to our economy? He is embarrassed about the deficits; he is embarrassed about the debt; he is embarrassed about the interest on the debt. Mr. President, there it is. Under whose Presidencies did that debt mushroom, like the prophet's gourd, overnight; from less than $1 trillion, from January 20, 1981, when President Reagan first took office, to $4,114 billion on March 1 of this year?

Tell the schoolchildren about that. Tell them when the deficits occurred. Tell them under whose administration those deficits occurred.

Mr. President, when those schoolchildren talk to the Senator from Missouri he is going to tell them about the interest on that debt, and rightly so. But the interest on the debt when Mr. Reagan took office was $69 billion in that year. And in fiscal year 1993 it is $198.7 billion. Almost $199 billion. Almost $200 billion.

So, Mr. President, tell those children—I hope the Senator will not be embarrassed to tell them when those deficits occurred, when that debt quadrupled, and when the interest on the debt rose from $69 billion to almost $200 billion.

That is a hidden tax, $200 billion a year. That is a hidden tax, a hidden tax. And it is caused by those burgeoning deficits that took place over the last 12 years—a hidden tax.

This President is trying to do something about that hidden tax. He is trying to reduce the budget deficits and eventually, in time, to reduce the debt and concomitantly, the interest on the debt. So I just hope what I said will be helpful to the distinguished Senator from Missouri when he faces those children who are— embarrassed about the deficits.

My grandchildren, my two daughters, and my two sons-in-law are embarrassed, too, about the debt. But I tell them how it rose. And the President, this President who has been in office just 73 days—73 days—is trying to do something about it. ...
...Let this President have a chance. Give him a chance. "

The Clinton economic plan, the 1993 Budget Reconciliation Act, was passed without a single Republican vote in either the House or the Senate. Vice President Gore's tie-breaking vote was required to pass the measure in the Senate on August 6, 1993, and President Clinton signed the legislation into law four days later.

Passage of the Clinton economic plan marked a major historic turning point. It reversed 12 years of supply-side economics, more commonly known as Reaganomics. In addition, it committed the nation to a path of fiscal discipline that ultimately erased the massive budget deficits. With the benefit of hindsight, let's look at the economic record of the Clinton administration.

In terms of the federal budget, the record $340.5 billion non-Social Security deficit in the last year of the Bush presidency was transformed into a record non-Social Security surplus of $86.4 billion in 2000.

The Republicans, who made it clear in 1993 that they did not want to be held responsible for the results of the Clinton economic package, began to sing a new tune when the results turned out to be just the opposite of what they had predicted. Former Vice President Dan Quayle probably spoke for most Republicans when he said. "We do have prosperity, but let's give credit where credit is due.

Ronald Reagan started the prosperity we have today. George Bush continued it, and Bill Clinton
inherited it."

A close look at the record shows just how inac-
curate Quayle's statement was. President Reagan
had the worst unemployment record of any modern
president. During his first four-year term, the average annual unemployment rate was 8.6 percent, and
the average annual unemployment rate for Reagan's
full 8-year presidency was 7.5 percent.

In terms of financial status, the national debt
doubled from $1 trillion to $2 trillion during the
first five years of the Reagan Presidency. It was
more than $2.6 trillion when Reagan left office, and
it had soared above the $4 trillion mark by the time
George H. W. Bush's 4-year presidency had ended.

Republicans have sought to deny President Clinton credit for the deficit reduction and the strong
economy during the Clinton years. After all, they
opposed his plan and did not contribute even one
Republican vote, in either the House or the Senate,
to the passage of the plan. Even worse, they were
adamant in their predictions that the plan would
devastate the economy and make the budget worse.

However, numerous experts, whose opinions
were far more important than those of partisan Republicans, gave Clinton high marks on his economic
and budgetary accomplishments. As early as the
fall of 1994, former federal Reserve Chairman, Paul
Volker wrote, "The deficit has come down, and I
give the Clinton Administration and President Clinton, himself, a lot of credit for that... and I think
we're seeing some benefits."

On February 20, 1996, Federal Reserve Chairman, Alan Greenspan, said the deficit reduction in the President's 1993 Economic plan was "an unquestioned factor in contributing to the improvement in economic activity that occurred thereafter."

According to the June 17, 1996 issue of *U.S. News and World Report*, "President Clinton's budget deficit program begun in 1993 (led) to lower interest rates, which begat greater investment growth (by double digits since 1993, the highest rate since the Kennedy administration), which begat three-plus years of solid economic growth, averaging 2.6 percent annually, 50 percent higher than during the Bush presidency."

All the above comments came after only 4 years of the Clinton administration. Any remaining doubt about the positive results of the Clinton economic program should have been erased during the President's second term.

During the Clinton years, the nation experienced the longest economic expansion in American history. More than 22 million new jobs were created in less than eight years, the most ever under a single administration. The unemployment rate dropped from 7 percent in 1993 when Clinton took office to 4 percent in November 2000. The overall unemployment rate was the lowest in 30 years, and the unemployment rate for women fell to the lowest rate in 40 years.

Credit for the strong economy during the Clinton years, and for the transformation of the budget from massive deficits to an $86.4 billion surplus in 2000, should go largely to the highly talented economic advisors that Clinton surrounded himself with, and ultimately to Clinton himself for listening to their advice and acting accordingly.

Just before his first inauguration, Clinton held an economic summit in Little Rock, at which business executives, financiers, and academics, one after another, moaned about how huge federal borrowing to cover debt was making capital too expensive to allow industry to grow. Clinton also put together a team of top economic advisers to help him chart a new course. But even more important than appointing talented economic advisers, Clinton was able to understand their advice, and he implemented much of it. Laura Tyson became chairperson of the Council of Economic Advisers. Bob Rubin, a widely respected financier, became Secretary of the Treasury, and Harvard Economist Lawrence Summers became Under Secretary of the Treasury. All of these people argued that the economic health of the nation required major reductions in the deficit.

Of course, this was not a new argument. Harvard economist, Martin Feldstein, who served as Reagan's Chairman of the Council of Economic Advisers, made the same argument to both Reagan and to the American people. However, Feldstein soon learned that his advice was not going to be taken seriously because it was in conflict with the political objectives of the Reagan administration.

President George Herbert Walker Bush also was advised to reduce the deficits by his economic advisers. However, implementing the advice of his economic advisers was in conflict with Bush's political objectives, so he chose to ignore them. Both Reagan and George H. W. Bush gave their own political objectives a higher priority than following sound economic policies. Most likely, President George H. W. Bush wished he had paid more attention to his economic advisers on the day he was defeated by Bill Clinton.

J. Bradford DeLong, an economist at the University of California at Berkeley was quoted in the February 2001 issue of *The Atlantic* as to the difference between Bill Clinton and his predecessors when it came to listening to economic advisers. Mr. DeLong wrote,

> "The difference between Bill Clinton and his predecessors lies not in the advice that he was given, but in the fact that he had the brains to understand it and the guts to follow through...Lifting the dead weight of the deficit from the economy cost him essentially all his political capital in 1993. And the rewards in terms of faster economic growth have been greater than anyone in 1993 would have dared predict...Economists will argue for decades to come over how much of the high-tech high productivity –growth boom we are currently experiencing is the result of the high-investment economy produced by the elimination of the deficit. It is a welcome change from the previous sport that academic economists played, that of assigning blame for relative stagnation."

Clinton's economic policies were based on the same traditional economic theory that had dominated American economic policy for more than forty years prior to the election of President Reagan. That theory, usually referred to as Keynesian economics, was named after the brilliant British economist, John Maynard Keynes whose monumental book, *The General Theory of Employment, Interest, and Money*, published in 1936, changed the way economists looked at the economy. Although his theories have undergone substantial refinement and revision, much of modern Keynesian economics is still rooted on the ideas set forth by Keynes.

Keynes argued that government should play an active role in maintaining the proper level of total spending in the economy in order to minimize both unemployment and inflation. He believed that with the proper use of the government's spending and taxing powers, the extremes of the business cycle could be avoided.

The size of the Gross Domestic Product (GDP), which is a measure of the total production of goods and services in the economy, is very important, in addition to the rate of growth of the GDP, because these two factors are the major determinants of the standard of living. If the GDP grows too slowly, or actually declines, there will be an increase in the number of people unemployed, whereas, if it grows too rapidly, increased inflation may occur.

The level of total production, and thus the level of employment, in the American economy is determined by the level of total spending (aggregate demand) for goods and services. American producers will produce just about as much as they can profitably sell. If sales fall off and inventories start to build up, a producer will lay off workers and curtail production to whatever level can be sold profitably. When sales pick up again and demand exceeds the current level of production, the producer will recall laid-off workers and expand production up to the point where production equals demand.

Thus, the key to a properly functioning economy is to maintain the proper level of total spending (aggregate demand) which is made up primarily of consumer spending, investment spending, and government spending. Through its spending and taxing powers, the government can have some control over the level of aggregate demand. If the economy is in a recession, with high unemployment, either increased government spending or increased consumer spending can help the economy to recover. A tax cut that puts additional take-home pay in the hands of consumers will almost certainly result in increased spending. However, it is especially important that the tax cut be temporary, and of the proper amount to stimulate the economy back to full employment without adding significantly to long-term deficits.

Most Keynesian economists believe that the government should aim for a roughly balanced budget over the long run. For example, over the course of the business cycle, the government's total spending should be approximately equal to its total revenue. During periods of recession and high unemployment, tax collections will decline and there will be an automatic increase in government spending for unemployment compensation and similar programs. However, as the economy recovers from the recession and laid-off workers return to work, there will be increased tax revenue and a decline in spending for unemployment compensation and similar programs. If Keynesian economic policies are followed consistently, there will be deficits in some years, and small surpluses in other years. Hopefully, over a period of years, the two would roughly balance out.

In addition to the automatic changes in government spending and tax collections that occur over the course of the business cycle, most Keynesian economists believe that the government should use temporary tax cuts to stimulate the economy during periods of recession and rising unemployment. What Keynesian economists do not support is large structural changes in the tax system that will lead to large budget deficits for years to come. That is why they were so opposed to the large permanent tax cuts under both Ronald Reagan and George W. Bush. Since there were no cuts in government spending to offset the lost revenue from the tax cuts, it was inevitable that the tax cuts would produce large budget deficits and a soaring national debt.

Keynesian economists are deeply concerned about the effect that massive federal borrowing has on interest rates. If businesses and consumers have to compete with the federal government for scarce funds, interest rates will inevitably rise. Higher interest rates discourage both business investment and consumer spending. Thus, ongoing large deficits alone can cause ongoing high unemployment.

President Clinton recognized the validity of Keynesian principles of economics, and he surrounded himself with competent economists who could advise him on proper government actions. The eight years of prosperity, and the transformation of massive deficits into a respectable surplus by 2000 were not accidental. The Clinton administration practiced sound economic policies, and the economy and the American people benefited enormously.

In short, both the budget and the economy were in great shape when Clinton turned over the reins of power to George W. Bush on January 20, 2001.

However, Bush chose to return to the failed economic policies of his father and Ronald Reagan that have very little support among professional economists. As a result, Bush more than offset the budgetary gains made during the Clinton years. Of course, the wars in Afghanistan and Iraq have had a big impact on the budget. But it was primarily the mismanagement of the economy and the federal budget, along with deregulation of the banking industry, that contributed to the financial meltdown in September 2008.

Despite his positive contributions to the economy and the federal budget, President Clinton must be faulted for the role he played in deceiving the American public about the true status of the federal budget. Like both George H. W. Bush who preceded him, and George W. Bush, his successor, Clinton continued to use the surplus in the Social Security fund to understate the true deficits in the government operating budget, and, once the budget was balanced, and we experienced two years of surpluses, he used the same accounting procedures to overstate the size of the surpluses.

Bill Clinton was the one who gave birth to the budget-surplus myth. He is the one who first proclaimed the "good news" about the federal government having excess money. Al Gore and George W. Bush both jumped on the bandwagon, and George W. Bush used the myth to get his huge, unaffordable tax cut enacted into law. But it is doubtful that the damaging Bush tax cuts could have been sold to the public without the reassurances of Bill Clinton that the government had huge surpluses when, in fact, the financial condition of the federal government was worse than it had ever been before.

There is also another area in which Clinton contributed to the colossal problems that the world now faces. In 1999, Clinton cooperated with Congressional Republicans in repealing the Glass-Steagall Act of 1933, a primary pillar of FDR's New Deal legislation that was designed to prevent a repeat of the 1930s financial collapse.

Under the Glass-Steagall Act, banks, brokerage firms, and insurance companies were effectively barred from entering each others' industries, and investment banking and commercial banking were separated. The repeal of Glass-Steagall opened the floodgates for mass mergers of companies in the financial industries. According to the *Wall Street Journal,* "With the stroke of the president's pen, investment firms like Merrill Lynch & Co., and banks like Bank of America Corp., are expected to be on the prowl for acquisitions." Although, much of the actual activity that led to the 2008 financial collapse occurred during the administration of George W. Bush, the flood gates were opened when Clinton signed the 1999 repeal of the Glass-Steagall Act.

CHAPTER FIVE

The Policies of George W. Bush

When George W. Bush became president on January 20, 2001, many economists were worried that his policies would have a negative impact on the economy and the federal budget. These fears turned out to be well founded. The nation was about to head into eight years of the most irresponsible and damaging economic policies in the history of the nation. During his last year, the catastrophic financial meltdown of 2008 occurred along with the worst world-wide recession since the Great Depression of the 1930s.

In addition to misrepresenting the financial status of the federal budget, President George W. Bush also misrepresented the potential economic effects of his proposed tax cut. On February 8, in an effort to stampede his tax cut through Congress, Bush suggested that the economy was headed for trouble which his tax cut could prevent. Speaking at a Rose Garden ceremony, Bush said, "A warning light is flashing on the dashboard of our economy. And we can't just drive on and hope for the best. We must act without delay." The president said his tax-cut proposal would "jump-start the economy," and he argued that swift passage of his plan by Congress could make the difference between growth and recession.

Many observers were shocked that a new president, who had been in office less than three weeks, would make such an irresponsible statement and risk spooking the markets and lowering consumer confidence. When Roosevelt became President during the depth of the Great Depression, he said, "The only thing we have to fear is fear itself," in an effort to calm the public and build optimism.

The fields of economics and psychology are so interwoven that if enough Americans come to believe that the nation is about to enter into a recession, their behavior will actually cause a recession. People will respond to their fears by cutting back on spending in preparation for anticipated layoffs, and as new orders to factories begin to decline, workers will indeed be laid off. Using scare tactics to get a tax cut enacted was inexcusable.

America was at a fork in the road in the year 2000. We could not go back and undo those terrible deficits. The weight of the $4.6 trillion that had been added to our national debt in the previous 19 years would have to be carried by the current and all future generations. But we did not have to add any significant new debt in the future. The tax structure and the government spending level were approximately in balance, and they would have remained in balance in the future unless we did something to throw them out of balance. It was a time to follow a stable economic course that was fiscally sound.

If the American people wanted to increase the level of government spending, then they would have had to be willing to support an increase in taxes to pay for that new spending. On the other hand, if the people collectively decided that they wanted a tax cut, they would also have to agree to a reduction in government spending equal to the reduction in taxes. By so doing, the nation's finances could have remained stable. We were stuck with the massive debt that we had accumulated in the past, and it would have been desirable for the government to set up a long-term plan for gradually paying down that debt. But, at the very least, we as a nation should have drawn a line in the sand that read, "NO ADDITIONAL DEBT."

The dire financial state the nation was in as a result of the large Reagan tax cuts, that were not matched by spending cuts, was crystal clear when President George H.W. Bush vacated the oval office. The beneficial effects of the Clinton deficit reduction package, which had totally eliminated the deficits by 1999, were equally clear. We, as a nation had gotten ourselves into deep financial trouble during the 12 years of Reagan-Bush, but we were in a position, in 2000, to chart a course that would avoid a repeat of past mistakes.

But George W. Bush was determined to return the nation to a new round of Reaganomics. He used the budget-surplus myth, created by Clinton, to convince the public that the government had massive amounts of surplus money which should be returned to the people in the form of tax cuts. There was no surplus money, and any tax cut would lead to new deficits unless offset by reduced spending.

Yet, Bush lied to the American people about the financial status of the government on a scale probably unprecedented in American history. He told enough lies to make Pinocchio's nose look short, and his performance as a con-artist rivaled that of Bernie Madoff.

Bush said, "My budget protects all $2.6 trillion of the Social Security surplus for Social Security, and for Social Security alone." However, Bush spent every dime of the Social Security surplus that came in during his eight years as president. He said he would pay down $2 trillion of the national debt. Instead, he added more than $5 trillion to the debt.

Americans always want to give a new president the benefit of any doubt, and they assume that the president is honorable and will take actions that are in the best interest of the country and the American people. They had no way of knowing that President Bush was lying to them. Economists and some members of Congress, including at least a few Republicans, were warning that enactment of the Bush tax cut would lead to a new round of huge budget deficits and resume the skyrocketing of the national debt. However, why should the public take the word of these people over that of their president?

Bush's actions in pushing through the 2001 tax cut were totally irresponsible. However, his actions to push through a second tax cut in 2003 require a stronger negative adjective. In 2003, President Bush betrayed the American people. By that time, it was quite clear just how great the negative impact of the 2001 tax cut had been on the budget and the economy. The non-Social Security deficit for fiscal 2002 had been a whopping $317.5 billion, and a

$467.6 billion deficit was being projected for fiscal 2003. Obviously, the $1.35 trillion tax cut of 2001 had affected the budget very differently than Bush had predicted.

With the out-of-control deficits, and the country fighting two wars with no end in sight, the 2001 tax cuts should have been rescinded before they did any more damage. It was time for the tax policy to be put in reverse. Instead, Bush called for still more of the same medicine that had already hurt the patient so badly.

In early 2003, Bush called for a large new tax-cut package. Economists were stunned. It seemed that George W. Bush was trying to undo all the fiscal gains that Clinton had made during his eight years. Remember that Clinton managed to totally eliminate the budget deficit during 1999 and 2000 and record the first two surpluses in 38 years. Although the national debt was a scary $5.6 trillion when Clinton left office, it was holding steady. By 2003, the debt was heading skyward again, setting off sirens in the minds of all those who cared about the fiscal solvency of the United States government.

What kind of mission was President George W. Bush on? Was he trying to sabotage both the economy and the budget of the country he was supposed to be leading? It was crazy, and the worst part of it all was that the American people, and the media, did not have a clue as to the almost certain consequences that would result from the actions. Because we were an economically illiterate nation, the people blindly followed President Bush down the pathway to economic catastrophe.

The nation's economists responded swiftly, in their vain effort to protect the economy and the budget. More than 400 of the nation's top economists, including 10 Nobel Laureates, signed a statement opposing the tax cut, and they placed a full-page ad in the *New York Times* to warn the public about the dangers of such action.

President Bush, who had revealed his ignorance of the field of economics, over and over, during his speeches, did more than ignore the economists. He arrogantly campaigned against them and anyone else who opposed his new tax cut. He tried to give the impression to the public that he knew better than the economists or anyone else what the economy needed. He traveled around the country giving speeches in which he urged voters to put pressure on members of Congress to vote for the tax cut.

On May 23, 2003, the United State Senate passed two pieces of legislation that are so contradictory that historians will be scratching their heads in an effort to figure out what could make the members of the Senate engage in such outrageous behavior. First, the Senate voted to raise the nation's legal debt limit by nearly $1 trillion, because in less than a week the Treasury was expected to run out of borrowing authority and risk default on the nation's debt. Secondly, on that same day, the Senate passed a $330 billion tax cut. If the financial condition of the United States government was so dire as to require almost a trillion-dollar increase in the debt ceiling, how could any senator justify voting for a $330 billion tax cut? The Senate ended up with a

50-50 tie vote, but Vice President Cheney cast the tie-breaking vote to pass the tax cut bill.

Today, the national debt has risen above the $11 trillion mark, and the financial fiasco has resulted in an apparent need for the government to spend massive amounts in bailout money. Where is that money going to come from? It will have to be borrowed, throwing the federal government still deeper in debt.

Historians may conclude that the American people must have suffered from some kind of mass insanity during the early 21st century. How else could they explain the fact that the public allowed their government to continue racing toward financial self-destruction? If they do their research well, the historians will figure out that there is a relatively simple explanation to the madness. It was a combination of economic ignorance on the part of the public, and willful deceit on the part of the government that resulted in the gross economic malpractice during the presidency of George W. Bush.

From the time of the Boston Tea Party to the present, Americans have hated taxes. They have begrudgingly paid enough taxes to keep the government afloat throughout most of the nation's history. However, the charismatic Ronald Reagan convinced the public that they were paying more taxes than was necessary and ushered in a new era in which tax resistance was greater than ever. Reagan delivered on his promise to dramatically reduce tax rates and give money back to the people. The tax cuts were like manna from heaven to the masses, and they reinforced the public's natural disdain for paying taxes. Therefore, when George W.

Bush once again told the public that the government was taking too much of the peoples' money and he wanted to give money back to them, they couldn't have been happier.

If the American people had been literate in economics, and if the media had reported the dismal financial status that the federal government was already in, there might not have been enough support to enact Bush's tax cuts. But most Americans have not had so much as a high school course in economics, and only a small percentage of journalists have been educated in the field.

This left the public helpless to stop the government malpractice. All they could do was to trust the elected government leaders to be truthful with them. And, when Bush extended a helping hand in the form of more tax cuts, the people happily accepted it.

They had no reason to believe their president was lying to them. Both President Clinton and Vice President Gore had said that the government had surplus money. How could the people possibly know that their trusted leaders were willfully lying to them for political reasons?

George W. Bush's campaign to partially privatize Social Security represented the ultimate depths to which he would descend in order to promote his conservative agenda. Conservatives have hated Social Security since the day it passed under Franklin D. Roosevelt in 1935, and they have been trying to destroy it ever since. Bush would have loved to have been the president who first began dismantling FDR's favorite program.

In early 2005, the Bush administration used great fanfare to announce a 60-day Social Security tour to promote Bush's partial privatization plan that would include at least 60 stops. The Bush people tried to bill the President's tour as a series of town hall meetings, but they were anything but traditional town hall meetings. They were staged and manipulated in such a way as to give the impression that everybody agreed with Bush's views on Social Security.

At the end of the 60 days, the campaign to privatize Social Security was extended indefinitely, and the campaign remained very active throughout the summer of 2005. However, when Hurricane Katrina struck the gulf coast in late August, coverage of the worst natural disaster in a century pushed most other topics, including Bush's Social Security campaign, out of the news for quite some time. Bush took such a beating from the press for his handling of the Katrina catastrophe that any momentum his Social Security privatization campaign might have built up was soon lost. Bush never resumed the Social Security crusade, so the issue just gradually faded out of the public consciousness.

Most Americans probably thought that Bush's Social Security proposal was something the president and his advisors had recently come up with. It was not. Bush was serving as an instrument of a group of conservative organizations which had hatched a plot to destroy Social Security, as we now know it, some 22 years earlier.

The playbook, upon which President Bush's strategy for privatizing Social Security was based was a proposal written in 1983 by Stuart Butler (a

Cato Director) and Peter Germanis (a policy analyst at the Heritage Foundation) and published in the *Cato Journal, vol. 3., no. 2* (Fall 1983). The title of the proposal was *"Achieving a Leninist' Strategy."* The article, outlining the plot, begins with a comparison of the views of Marx and Lenin with regard to the belief that capitalism was doomed by its inherent contradictions. According to Butler and Germanis, Marx believed that capitalism would inevitably collapse on its own. However, Lenin wanted to mobilize an alliance, both to hasten the collapse and to ensure that the result conformed with his interpretation of the proletarian state. Butler and Germanis write that, "Unlike many other socialists at the time, Lenin recognized that fundamental change is contingent both upon a movement's ability to create a focused political coalition and upon its success in isolating and weakening its opponents."

Butler and Germanis urged the adoption of a similar strategy for reforming Social Security. They write,

> "As we contemplate basic reform of the Social Security system, we would do well to draw a few lessons from the Leninist strategy. Many critics of the present system believe as Marx and Lenin did of capitalism, that the system's days are numbered because of its contradictory objectives of attempting to provide both welfare and insurance. All that really needs to be done, they contend, is to point out these inherent flaws to the taxpayers and to show them that Social Security would be vastly improved if it were restructured into a predominantly private system."

Butler and Germanis advocate a specific set of plans for accomplishing the goal of replacing the existing Social Security system with a private system. They write, "By approaching the problem in this way, we may be ready for the next crisis in Social Security—ready with a strong coalition for change, a weakened coalition supporting the current system, and a general public familiar with the private-sector option."

All of the elements of the 2005 Bush crusade are spelled out in the 1983 playbook, or "plot book," and it was clear that the Bush administration was going by the book of the Cato Institute. Every element of the Bush strategy was an exact match for the recommendations that were published in the Cato Journal in 1983 under the title, *"Achieving A 'Leninist' Strategy."*

The final paragraph of "Achieving a 'Leninist' Strategy," illustrates the resolve and determination by the conservatives to someday completely dismantle the Social Security program and replace it with a privatized system. It reads:

> "Finally, we must be prepared for a long campaign. The next Social Security crisis may be further away than many people believe. Or perhaps it will occur before the reform coalition is strong enough to achieve a political breakthrough. In either case, it could be many years before the conditions are such that a radical reform of Social Security is possible. But then, as Lenin well knew, to be a successful revolutionary, one must also be patient and consistently plan for real reform."

These revolutionaries must have been very disappointed that the 1983 Social Security "fix" worked as well as it did. They apparently got tired of waiting for a real Social Security crisis to come along and decided to convince George W. Bush to create such a crisis.

The conservatives and libertarians, with George W. Bush as their spokesman, activated the "Leninist Strategy" in 2005 precisely because they did not see any real Social Security crisis on the horizon. With the re-election of President George W. Bush, and with Republican control of the Congress, they were gambling that they could fool the American public, and pull off their revolution, even in the absence of a real Social Security crisis.

It is possible that if Hurricane Katrina had not struck when it did, and if Bush's public approval rating had been higher, he might have been successful in getting his Social Security proposal enacted into law. Although he did not succeed, I am troubled by the fact that most Americans don't know, and may never know, the sinister nature of what President George W. Bush was trying to pull off. He was trying to ram down the throats of the American people a plan formulated by a small minority of right-wing Americans who had conspired to use deception and guerrilla warfare to destroy a program that was so popular that it could not be brought down through the normal democratic process.

Hopefully, the Wall Street Meltdown has shown just how dangerous and expensive it can be to allow government and business officials to mislead the public. We cannot afford to allow this charade to continue anymore. For more than a quarter century, the American people have been deliberately deceived by their leaders. The people, and the nation as a whole, have been severely injured by this practice.

Ronald Reagan and George W. Bush brought about many changes in America and left a legacy of huge budget deficits and a soaring national debt. But both failed to achieve the goal that was probably most dear to their hearts—the dismantling of the federal government as we know it. The hidden agenda of these two presidents as well as many of their conservative supporters was to dramatically downsize the role of government in the American economy. They hated big government and were determined to bring about a major downsizing. They had a plan that they thought would accomplish that goal. The plan was to cut taxes by so much that when the deficits began to soar, Congress would be forced to dismantle major government programs. They would cut off the life blood to the social programs they despised so much, thus starving them to death. Ronald Reagan made his intentions very clear in his first televised address to the nation on February 5, 1981. Reagan declared:

"We can lecture our children about extravagance until we run out of voice and breath. Or we can cut their extravagance by simply reducing their allowance."

Reagan seemed to think he could cut government spending by simply reducing taxes and thus cutting back on the government's "allowance," but he underestimated the determination of members of Congress to spend on programs they believed in

whether the revenue was there or not. And Reagan
was unwilling to cut back on defense spending. So
the reduction in tax revenue, resulting from the big
Reagan tax cuts, was not offset by similar reductions in spending. The national debt quadrupled
during the Reagan-Bush years, but spending continued, and the deficit during the last year of George
Herbert Walker Bush's presidency was an all time
record of $340.5 billion.

With the election of Bill Clinton in 1992, the attempt to downsize the federal government ended.
The Clinton deficit-reduction package gradually
eliminated the huge deficits, and Clinton actively
tried to make government a more responsive servant
to the American people. He even pursued a controversial campaign to establish a national health care
system at the beginning of his first term, but failed
to get it enacted into law.

Al Gore strongly believed that the government
should play an active role in improving the lives of
American citizens and, if he had been elected in
2000, we would have seen increased spending on
both education and health care programs during his
administration. With the election so close that the
outcome was ultimately decided by the United
States Supreme Court, and given the fact that Gore
received more popular votes than Bush, it would be
hard for anyone to make a strong rational argument
that Bush had a mandate from the people to bring
about major changes in America.

Since he clearly did not have a mandate for
any major change in United States policy, it would
have been impossible for George W. Bush to launch
a direct open campaign to downsize the govern-

ment. He would not have been able to get the support of either the Congress or the American people for such action. But getting public support for major tax cuts was a different story, and Bush saw this as an alternative route to dismantling big government.

Like Reagan, George W. Bush was no fan of the federal government. Like most conservative governors, George W. Bush, as governor of Texas, came to despise the restraints placed on state government by the federal government. His decision to seek the presidency must have been at least partly motivated by his desire to trim the size of the federal government. In order to get elected he needed the support of the ultra conservative wing of the Republican party as well as the Christian Coalition and other Christian right organizations.

Bush used the term "Compassionate Conservatism" to describe his right wing agenda. These two words contradict each other. There is nothing compassionate about true conservative ideology. Over the years, conservatives have consistently opposed programs to help the poor and the disadvantaged. They have opposed programs designed to provide greater equality of opportunity. They have favored cutting benefits to the disadvantaged in order to provide tax cuts to the rich, and they have been more concerned about the profits of large corporations than about the incomes of ordinary Americans.

Compassionate Conservatism was just another Trojan horse, another method of deceit to bring about change that the people would not support on its own merits. Bush was determined to impose his own views and those of right-wing conservatives upon the American people no matter how much fraud was required to accomplish the task. In a speech in San Jose, California on April 30, 2002, Bush revealed his desire for limited government. Excerpts from the speech are reproduced below.

"We are a generous and caring people. We don't believe in a sink-or-swim society. The policies of our government must heed the universal call of all faiths to love a neighbor as we would want to be loved our-selves. We need a different approach than either big government or indifferent government. We need a government that is focused, effective, and close to the people; a government that does a few things, and does them well."

There was no mistaking Bush's view of the role of government. When he said, "We need a gov-ernment ...that does a few things and does them well," he was signaling his intention to trim the size and scope of government. Bush went on to explain his philosophy of "compassionate conservatism:"

"Government cannot solve every problem, but it can en-courage people and communities to help themselves and to help one another. Often the truest kind of compassion is to help citizens build lives of their own. I call my philosophy and approach "compassionate conservatism." It is compas-sionate to actively help our fellow citizens in need. It is con-servative to insist on responsibility and on results. And with this hopeful approach we can make a real difference in peo-ple's lives."

Bush's approach was nothing more than having the government turn its back on the most disadvan-taged Americans and calling it compassionate. The conservative portion of the approach was taking the money targeted for programs for the poor and giving it to the rich in the form of tax cuts.

So what was the real reason for the huge Bush tax cuts? It was certainly not because they would help the economy or the budget. They harmed both the economy and the budget. It was not because the government had surplus money. The government had never been so deep in debt. I believe the tax cuts were a deliberate effort to put the finances of the United States Government in such dire straights that Congress would be forced to dismantle the social safety net. I believe the purpose of the tax cuts was to intentionally create a financial crisis unlike anything the United States had ever before faced. Under such conditions, it might be possible for the conservatives to accomplish things that they could never accomplish through the democratic process.

The Reagan tax cuts created a situation where the tax system was not capable of generating enough revenue to balance the budget under any circumstances. The Clinton deficit reduction package partially fixed the problem. In 1999 and 2000, when the economy was operating at the peak of the business cycle, with the lowest unemployment rate in 30 years, the nation was able to experience non-Social Security surpluses for the first time in 38 years. However, in 2001, as the economy slipped into recession the deficits returned.

In short, before George W. Bush took office and began pursuing tax cuts, the tax rates were already insufficient to generate a balanced budget except under extraordinary circumstances. There was no wiggle room for even small tax cuts. If tax rates had been left as they were, the government would probably still have run deficits in most years. However, those deficits would have been small enough that they would not have posed a major threat to the budget or economic stability. But even a small reduction in tax rates would have almost guaranteed budget deficits in each and every year.

At the time Bush took over the reins of government, the economy was performing very well with unemployment at historic lows. There was still the fact that the national debt had increased from $1 trillion in 1981 to more than $6 trillion by 2001. However, because there were budget surpluses in both 1999 and 2000, the national debt was not growing at the time Clinton left office.

Bush inherited a healthy economy, and the budget deficits that had plagued the nation since the Reagan administration had finally been brought under control by Clinton. The old expression, "Don't fix it if it ain't broke," applied to the American economy as we entered the new century more than ever before. Yet, Bush seemed determined to break the economy so that it would need to be fixed. Despite widespread opposition, he pushed his 2001 $1.35 trillion tax cut through, promising that it would not mean a return to deficits, or the pirating of any of the Social Security surplus.

By 2003, it was clear that both the economy and the budget outlook had deteriorated instead of improving as Bush had predicted. The 2002 non-Social Security deficit was a whopping $317.5 billion, and the projected deficit for 2003 was $467.6 billion. Instead of admitting that he was wrong, and calling for repeal of the 2001 tax cut, Bush called for a new tax cut.

This time there was no claim that the government had surplus money with which to fund the tax cut. Instead, Bush claimed the tax cut would stimulate the economy and create jobs. Bush knew that the proposed tax cut would create few new jobs and that it would lead to even higher deficits. But what did that matter? It would just speed up the impending crisis which would enable him to dismantle the government social programs he despised so much.

Such a day of reckoning was bound to come. As the deficits become larger and larger, and the government had to borrow more and more money, interest rates would be forced up. Higher interest rates would serve as a drag on the economy and lead to higher unemployment. As the unemployment rose and fewer Americans had jobs, government tax revenue would decline even more, and automatic government spending programs such as unemployment compensation would rise. This would result in even larger deficits.

It is hard to find any rationalization for the unaffordable Bush tax cuts other than that they would "starve the federal government" and require major spending cuts. Since defense spending was not a likely candidate for cutbacks, and interest on the national debt must be paid in order for the government to be able to continue to borrow, spending cuts would most likely fall upon Social Security, Medicare, health programs and public education.

Since the large surpluses resulting from the 1983 Social Security tax increase, and specifically earmarked for funding the retirement of the baby boomers, have already been borrowed by the government and spent on other programs, there will be a terrible crunch in both the Social Security and Medicare programs. Unless the government raises taxes in order to repay the massive amounts of money that it has borrowed from these funds, there will have to be major cutbacks in both Social Security and Medicare benefits.

The attempt to eliminate social programs, by cutting off their funding source by devious means, is the granddaddy of all frauds. It violates everything that American democracy stands for. It is the people—not the president—who hold the power to decide what programs they want and how much in taxes they are willing to pay for these programs. It is the people, through their elected representatives, who decide the appropriate role of government. And it is the people who have the authority to choose whether to role back the pages of time and return to an era long ago rejected by the majority of Americans, or to move forward to an era where the American dream is possible for more and more Americans.

There is no such thing as liberal or conservative economics. Any good economist could design a set of sound economic policies for either a liberal or a conservative administration. The most basic principle that both plans would have in common is that the government should not spend more than it receives in revenue over the long run. Historically, most budget deficits have been caused by increases in government spending that were not matched by corresponding tax increases. By contrast, the massive $10 trillion increase in the national debt, just since 1981, has come mostly from tax cuts that were not matched by spending cuts.

CHAPTER SIX

Tax Cuts and Job Creation

If you say something that people want to believe enough times, people begin to believe it. For example, back during the days of the budget-surplus myth, the American people were told over and over that the government had huge amounts of surplus money. They were told by Bill Clinton, Al Gore, George W. Bush, and many members of Congress. Journalists just seemed to accept the myth as true so they passed the good news on to everyone who would listen. Almost everybody got into the act, and organizations began running ads lobbying for part of the loot.

Of course, we know today that there was never any significant true surplus except for the temporary planned surpluses in the Social Security program that resulted from the 1983 Social Security tax increase. This money was specifically earmarked for the funding of the retirement of the baby-boom generation, and was not supposed to be used for any purpose other than paying Social Security benefits. The tiny $1.9 billion non-Social Security surplus of 1999 and the larger surplus of $86.4 billion in 2000 were the only non-Social Security surpluses of the past 40 years, and they were not even large enough to offset the deficits of 1997 and 1998.

The whole budget surplus fantasy was a hoax against the American people. Essentially, it was a very **BIG LIE** told by many people. Some of them may have been so poorly informed about the budget situation that they actually believed what they were saying. But not the top leadership. They willfully and knowingly deceived the American public.

Another lie is that tax cuts of any kind stimulate the economy and result in the creation of many jobs. Tax cuts that put money into the hands of consumers who are not buying because they are unemployed, or because they are on a very tight budget, can stimulate the economy and create jobs. However, tax cuts that go to the super rich, who already have almost everything that money can buy, will have little or no positive effect on the economy or job creation. They will, however, lead to large budget deficits and a soaring national debt.

When the economy is in a recession, with high levels of unemployment, the most effective way of giving the economy a boost is to put money into the hands of consumers who make up more than two-thirds of the total demand in the economy. The simplest and most effective way to accomplish this goal is through temporary one-time tax rebates. For example, a check for $500, might be sent to each American taxpayer, most of whom would probably spend the rebate. Since it is a one-time rebate, and tax rates are not changed, it would have a very limited effect on deficits over the long run. It would give the economy a jump start which is all that is needed to stimulate it out of recession.

If the primary goal of the tax rebate is to improve the economy, and policy makers don't get all caught up in the politics of who should get how much in terms of fairness, a strong case can be made for targeting most of the tax rebate to those people in the lowest income brackets who will spend almost 100 percent of the rebate on consumer goods and services.

As consumer spending increases, and new orders begin coming into factories, the employers will begin calling back laid-off workers so they can increase production. When the newly recalled workers begin getting paychecks again, they will increase their spending, causing still more unemployed workers to be recalled. This process can continue until the economy once again reaches full employment. If the first tax rebate is not sufficient stimulus, then another rebate can be used to complete the job.

When consumer demand is high, employers hire additional workers in order to fill the demand. This is the way that jobs get created. The Bush position that you should give tax breaks to businesses so they will create jobs is just plain wrong. No amount of tax relief for businesses will cause them to create jobs if they cannot sell their products. Demand is what creates jobs. If a company has such strong demand for its products that it is turning away customers for lack of inventory, you can be absolutely sure that it will expand its productive capacity to meet the demand, and not a penny of government tax relief is necessary for them to do this.

Tax cuts for the rich may be good politics for a president who gets much of his financial support from such people, but it is lousy economics. Rich people don't have a lot of unmet needs that they will fill only if they get a tax cut. Most of them already have almost everything they want, in terms of material goods and services, so when the rich get a tax cut they usually just turn it over to their accountant with instructions to find a good place to invest it. One of those "good places to invest" is with the United States Treasury.

Because of the tax cuts during the Reagan-Bush administrations, and those under George W. Bush, the national debt has soared beyond anything that any reasonable person could have imagined at the time that Reagan first became President. The government must constantly finance and refinance this huge debt by borrowing. Since the government has to finance the deficits, no matter how high the interest rate, it will always be competing with businesses and consumers for funds. This competition tends to drive interest rates up over the long run.

What happens to a lot of the money that the rich receive in the form of big tax cuts is that they loan it right back to the government and earn interest on it by investing it in United States Treasury notes and bonds. Money that was coming in to the government in the form of tax revenue before, now comes in the form of borrowed money on which interest must be paid. The key point here is that large tax cuts to the rich play almost no role in the creation of new jobs. For tax cuts to stimulate the economy and create jobs, they must result in new spending for goods and services.

The idea of cutting tax rates permanently at a time when tax revenue falls far short of expenditures is almost suicidal. It makes no economic sense whatsoever. When you jump start your car with another battery, once the engine starts, you remove the secondary battery. Jump starting the economy should work the same way. You need a one-time jolt in the form of a tax rebate, and then the economy takes off on its own. If the first jolt is not sufficient to stimulate the economy back to the full-employment level, you can always give it another jolt with another rebate, but it is foolhardy to cut long-term tax rates unless you are willing to cut long-term government spending by a similar amount. The deficits that result from the tax cuts require additional government borrowing which can drive interest rates up and reduce business investment spending because of the higher interest rates. If this happens, jobs can be lost because of this particular type of tax cut.

The notion that cutting tax rates can result in increased revenue is nonsense. If your boss tells you that he is going to increase your income by cutting your wage rate, you probably are going to see through the gimmick. Given the same number of hours worked, a lower wage rate means less earnings, whereas a higher wage rate results in increased earnings. Likewise, lower tax rates mean less tax revenue, and higher tax rates mean more revenue.

This can be seen clearly by what happened during the 1980s after the Reagan tax cut and what happened during the 1990s, as a result of the Clinton deficit-reduction package which included higher tax rates. The Reagan tax cuts led to massive budget deficits and a quadrupling of the national debt in just 12 years. The Clinton deficit-reduction package led to a gradual elimination of budget deficits with actual budget surpluses in 1999 and 2000.

George W. Bush then pushed through another big tax cut, and we returned to large annual deficits. Forget about the supply-siders' theory that cuts in tax rates generate increased revenue. The theory has been tested and the results are indisputable. No amount of fuzzy math can show that lower tax rates resulted in higher revenue than would have been the case if the rates had been left unchanged.

Some die-hard Reaganites present numbers showing tax collections higher a few years after the Reagan tax cut than they were at the time the rates were cut and offer that as "proof" that the tax cuts resulted in higher revenue. Nice try, but they forgot something. Our economy should be growing continuously over time as the population increases and more productive resources become available. With a growing labor force, and more workers paying taxes, there should be a substantial growth in revenue. Even when tax rates are cut, this ongoing growth in the economy will more than offset the rate cut and revenue will increase gradually even at the lower rates.

The point is that revenue would have increased a great deal more without the tax cuts. In short, tax revenue did grow in the years after the Reagan tax cuts, but it did not grow nearly as fast as it would have grown, if the tax cuts had not taken place. The revenue did not rise because of the tax cuts. It rose despite the tax cuts because of the general growth in the population and the overall economy.

By the same token, the natural growth in the population and the economy over time also results in higher government expenditures. Unless the growth in revenue keeps pace with the growth in expenditures, budget deficits will occur. It is precisely because the growth in revenue did not keep pace with the growth in expenditures after the Reagan tax cuts that the huge deficits occurred and the national debt rose from less than $1 trillion when Reagan took office to more than $4 trillion by the time George Herbert Walker Bush vacated the White House.

Likewise, it is precisely because of the deficit reduction package implemented early in the Clinton presidency that deficits were gradually reduced during his first six years and were replaced by surpluses in 1999 and 2000. And it is partly because of the reduction in interest rates, made possible by the deficit reductions, that the economy was able to experience the longest period of prosperity in American history during the Clinton years.

It should have been clear to all candidates, in 2000, that cutting taxes without cutting spending was a recipe for disaster. When Reagan had tried it, in 1981, the national debt quadrupled from $1 trillion to $4 trillion in just 12 years. Why would anyone want a repeat of that performance? Of course, the public was told that the federal budget situation was different in 2000 than it had been in 1981. According to President Clinton, Al Gore, George W. Bush, and many others, something wonderful had mysteriously happened to the federal government. It had stumbled upon a treasure chest full of surplus money.

Nobody even bothered to ask the question, "How could that be?" Never before in American history had the government come upon such a windfall. How could it be that, at the very time when both candidates for president needed a budget surplus to exist in order to justify their campaign promises, the hoped for surplus just magically appeared out of thin air? People have a tendency to "never question a good thing." If the president and both candidates said the government had surplus money, it must be true. And, if it were true, maybe the tax cut would turn out differently than it had turned out under Reagan when there was no surplus money.

The American people, who were almost totally illiterate in the area of economics, were the victims of unforgivable fraud by the Bush administration. The Bush people lied to the public in order to enact both the 2001 tax cut and the 2003 cut. In 2001, the people were told that the reason for the tax cut was that the government had surplus money resulting from over-taxation and that the cut would only re-turn the surplus money to the taxpayers. They were assured that there would be no return to deficits and that the Social Security money would not be touched. The **BIG LIE** in 2001 was that there was surplus revenue to fund the tax cut.

By 2003, it should have been clear to everyone that the 2001 tax cut had inflicted serious damage on both the federal budget and the economy. The talk of fantasy surpluses had given way to the real-ity that we were once again operating deep in deficit territory. So when Bush decided to try to push through another large tax cut in 2003, he knew the public would no longer buy the lie that there were surplus dollars to pay for it. Instead, he would have to concoct a new lie in order to sell the second tax cut.

The **BIG LIE** that Bush chose to use to sell his 2003 tax cut was to claim that the new tax cut would solve the high unemployment problem. He gave the new proposal the nickname of "Job Creation Program." and sold it as a remedy for the high unemployment. The Bush tax cut was not a job creation program. It was an attempt to restructure the tax system to favor the rich. Like all such political proposals, in order to make the proposal more palatable, a few crumbs were included that would also benefit lower income families. But these portions were so small that they would do little to stimulate the economy.

This point was made strongly by more than 400 of the nation's top economists. They signed a statement, adamantly opposing the proposal, which appeared as a full-page ad in the *New York Times*. Excerpts from the statement are reproduced below:

"...Regardless of how one views the specifics of the Bush plan, there is wide agreement that its purpose is a permanent change in the tax structure and not the creation of jobs and growth in the near-term...

...Passing these tax cuts will worsen the long-term budget outlook, adding to the nation's projected chronic deficits. This fiscal deterioration will reduce the capacity of the government to finance Social Security and Medicare benefits as well as investments in schools, health, infrastructure, and basic research. Moreover, the proposed tax cuts will generate further inequalities in after-tax income.

> To be effective, a stimulus plan should rely on immediate but temporary spending and tax measures to expand demand, and it should also rely on immediate but temporary incentives for investment. Such a stimulus plan would spur growth and jobs in the short term without exacerbating the long-term budget outlook."

Economists have long been criticized by government officials for their lack of agreement on certain basic issues. This practice started with President Harry Truman who said, "I am looking for a one handed economist. My economists keep telling me 'On the one hand this might be the right way to go, but on the other hand...'" President Truman wanted an economist who saw everything as black or white with no areas of gray. The problem is that there are few issues in economics that are so clear cut that everything is black or white.

Given this reality, it is amazing that 400 economists were able to agree on the wording of a statement that they could all sign. If the economists agreed that the effect of the Bush plan would be a permanent change in the tax structure that would generate further inequalities in after-tax income and not the creation of jobs and growth in the near-term, there was a very high probability that they were right.

What is the likelihood that George W. Bush would know more about any field than the top 400 experts in that field? What is the probability that George W. Bush was correct, and the 400 economists were wrong, about the potential job creation of the Bush plan? I think that any reasonable person would agree that there was almost zero chance that Bush was right and the economists were wrong.

One of the traits of truly intelligent and wise people is that they realize that they can always learn from experts in any field because the experts have dedicated their lives, and years of study, to that field. It is hard to imagine any person risking his or her future by going against all the accumulated knowledge and the advice of most of the experts in any field. It is the ultimate in outrageous, irresponsible behavior, for a president of the United States to risk the future of the American people by defiantly and deliberately going against the advice of top experts.

Most Americans were probably never aware of the position and advice of the economists despite the fact that the statement appeared in the New York Times. It received very little national news coverage relative to the coverage President Bush got when he traveled around the country urging people to pressure their representatives in Congress to support his tax bill because it would create jobs.

The president did not tell the public that most economists were opposed to the plan. He also did not tell them that the plan would greatly benefit the rich at the expense of America's future. He used one theme. This bill is about the creation of jobs. A vote for this bill is a vote for jobs.

Despite the fact that two million jobs had already been lost since Bush took office, Americans who trusted the president to tell the truth supported the bill. But even some highly respected Republican members of the Senate, who probably did not trust the president to do what was best for America, opposed the measure. After much arm-twisting and the deliberate deception of the American people as to what the bill would really do, Bush managed to get his tax cut through Congress with the tie-breaking vote of Vice President Cheney.

Enactment of both the 2001 and the 2003 Bush tax cuts were accomplished only by engaging in fraud against the American people. Fraud is very broadly defined for purposes of both civil and criminal litigation. An excerpt from the article on fraud in Encyclopedia Americana is reproduced below.

> "Generally fraud involves the intentional mis-representation of a material fact, resulting in dam-age to the victim. So defined, fraud may form the basis of a civil action for damages or of a criminal prosecution...Although fraud is often perpetrated by means of actual statements that misrepresent facts, deception that constitutes fraud can be prac-ticed by concealment, by half –truths calculated to deceive, or tricks or devices that mislead the vic-tim. Also, a statement made recklessly without knowing its truth or falsity may, if false, constitute a fraud."

Certainly Bush's actions in pushing both tax bills through Congress fell under the criteria of fraud as defined above. The President pushed the 2001 tax cut on the basis of alleged large surpluses as far as the eye could see. There were no such surpluses, and the President had to know this by the time his proposal came up for a vote. He was clearly guilty of "intentional misrepresentation of a material fact resulting in damage to the victim." The victim in this case was the millions of Americans who were adversely affected by repercussions of the tax cut.

Bush was equally guilty of fraud in his campaign to get the 2003 tax cut enacted. In this case, he did not claim that there was surplus money to fund it. Instead, he came up with a new lie about the job-creation potential of the cut. He knew that the 400 plus economists who signed the statement opposing the cut were correct in their contention that it would do little to create jobs. Yet, he deliberately set out to undermine the experts and get the tax cut passed based on the lie that it was a job-creation bill.

In summary, the Bush tax cuts of 2001 and 2003 caused massive additional deficits and pushed the size of the national debt to astronomical new levels. The tax cuts created additional inequalities in after-tax incomes, and they did little to create jobs. Bush could have used one-time tax rebates to restore the economy to full employment at only a tiny fraction of the cost of the tax cuts that were passed, and such one-time rebates would have had little negative effect on the long-term budget outlook.

Bush chose to push the tax cuts through, not in an effort to help the economy, but because the tax cuts were an integral part of his hidden agenda to greatly reduce the size and scope of the federal government. Reagan had tried to starve the government into becoming much leaner by cutting off part of the revenue flow with his big tax cuts. However, Reagan's plan backfired. Instead of decreasing spending by the amount of the tax cuts, Congress chose to replace the lost tax revenue by borrowing and increasing the size of the national debt. Instead of the "tax and spend" policies that Democrats were so often accused of, the Republicans chose to launch a new era that would follow the policy of "borrow and spend."

For 20 of the past 28 years (12 years under Reagan-Bush and 8 years under George W. Bush) the American economy has operated under policies that did not have the support of most mainstream economists. Indeed, except for the Clinton years, professional economists have played little role in basic economic policymaking for the past 28 years.

Both Ronald Reagan and George W. Bush pushed through large tax cuts that were not matched by corresponding cuts in government spending. In both cases, the results were catastrophic in terms of runaway deficits and a skyrocketing national debt. However, I believe that historians may be harsher on George W. Bush than they will be on Ronald Reagan for initiating the tax cuts.

It appears that Ronald Reagan actually believed that his tax cut would work the way his advisers told him it would work. It was based on a new theory that had never been tested. As absurd as it was, that theory predicted that lower tax rates would somehow lead to higher tax revenue. If the theory had worked out in practice, the tax cuts would not have led to large deficits.

The charismatic Reagan was able to convince the public that the theory would work. Given these circumstances, perhaps historians will forgive Reagan for his early faulty judgment. However, when the tax cuts led to a doubling of the national debt, from $1 trillion to $2 trillion, in just five years, Reagan should have sought repeal of the tax cuts. The supply-side theory had been tested, and it had flunked the test. The continuation of the same policy for the next seven years under Reagan-Bush is what is unforgivable.

The effects of the Reagan tax cuts were clear. After 12 years of Reaganomics, the national debt had quadrupled to $4 trillion. Bill Clinton promised to eliminate the huge deficits if he were elected president. Clinton delivered on that promise. His deficit-reduction package, which included both spending cuts and higher taxes, led to a gradual decline in the annual deficits during his first six years in office, and to a complete elimination of the deficits in 1999 and 2000. During those final two years, the government ran surpluses in the budget after 38 consecutive years of deficits.

In a sense, a national experiment measuring the relationship between tax rates and budget deficits was conducted during the 20-year period 1981-2001. During the first 12 years the economy operated under Reaganomics with large cuts in tax rates. During the last 8 years, the economy operated under traditional economic policies based on Keynesian theory and Clinton's deficit reduction program.

During the 12-year period of Reagan-Bush, we had ballooning deficits and a quadrupling of the national debt. During the 8-year period that the economy operated using traditional economy theory, the deficits got progressively smaller during the first six years and were eliminated, and replaced by surpluses, during 1999 and 2000.

The information gathered during the entire 20-year period did not surprise mainstream economists who had opposed Reaganomics in the first place. But it did give an opportunity for the supply-side theorists to test their theories. The evidence was clear. During the Reagan-Bush years, tax rates were too low to generate enough revenue to balance the budget, no matter how well the economy performed. Under the Clinton tax structure, rates were not high enough to balance the budget during the first six years of his presidency. However, once the economy boomed at the peak of the business cycle, the deficits were replaced by small surpluses.

Under the Clinton tax structure, rates were still not high enough to balance the budget in most years, given the level of government spending at the time. Therefore, sound economic policy in 2001 would have dictated either additional cuts in government spending, or a small increase in tax rates so the economy would have had the capacity to balance the federal budget in most years.

That is where the economy stood during the 2000 presidential election campaign. Although tax rates were too low to generate enough revenue to balance the budget in most years, the nation could have lived with the small deficits that would have occurred during the years when the economy was operating in the low phase of the business cycle. In a sense, it was a classic case of "the economy ain't broke so don't fix it."

The above statement is based on the assumption that people were satisfied with the level of government services that were affordable under the current tax structure. In other words, the public was content to have the government hold the line on government expenditures. Any increase in government expenditures would have to be offset by corresponding increases in taxes. On the other hand, any decrease in tax rates would have had to be offset by equal cuts in government spending. You didn't have to be an economist to understand this fact. After 38 years of consecutive budget deficits, in 1999 and 2000, the government operated without budget deficits.

The only sane way to operate any budget, whether it is an individual household budget, a business budget, or the budget of any unit of government, is to aim to keep spending within the bounds of income. Sure there will be years when spending exceeds income, but these years should be offset by other years during which spending is less than income. It doesn't take a great deal of intelligence, or education, to understand the basic concept that you cannot indefinitely spend more than the amount of your income.

Yet, throughout the 2000 presidential campaign, both George W. Bush and Al Gore promised to both cut taxes and increase government spending. This was crazy, and I think historians will give both candidates low marks for their proposed economic programs. If Al Gore had been elected, instead of George W. Bush, some things would have certainly been different. But, with regard to economic policy, if Gore had carried out his campaign promises to increase spending and cut taxes, the nation would have still experienced huge budget deficits and a skyrocketing national debt.

The promises of both Bush and Gore were based on a very **BIG LIE**. They both told the American people that the government had billions of dollars of surplus money with which to finance these promises. They used the budget-surplus myth that Bill Clinton had given birth to, as a campaign vehicle

that would allow them to see who could out-
promise the other during the campaign. I have a
great deal of respect for former Vice President Al
Gore and the good work he is doing with regard to
the environment. However, I cannot respect him for
lying to the American people, along with Bill Clinton and George W. Bush, about the mythical budget
surplus.

These lies enabled President George W. Bush to
sabotage the American economy and the federal
budget, and they played a key role in contributing to
the current crises and the suffering of people around
the world.

CHAPTER SEVEN

The Financial Status of the U.S. Government

"The practical implications of this is bankruptcy for the United States," Republican Senator Judd Gregg of New Hampshire said on Sunday, March 22, 2009, during a CNN appearance. Senator Gregg was referring to the Obama administration's recently released budget proposal.

"If we maintain the proposals that are in this budget over the ten-year period that this budget covers," Gregg continued, "This country will go bankrupt. People will not buy our debt, our dollar will become devalued."

These were harsh words, coming from the Republican Senator who was offered, but turned down, the post of Obama's Secretary of Commerce. However, Senator Gregg is known as one of the keenest fiscal minds on Capitol Hill, so nobody took his warning lightly.

News coverage of the world banking crisis and the severe recession, has been so extensive that these problems have become almost common knowledge. However, the financial problems of the United States government, which have been more than two decades in the making, are not well known.

As pointed out previously, the national debt reached the $1 trillion mark for the very first time in early 1981. This $1 trillion represented the cumulative budget deficits of all previous presidents. At that rate of growth, the national debt did not pose a significant problem for our government, and if the debt had continued to grow only at that rate, it would never have posed such a problem. But things changed dramatically. The national debt doubled in just five years, and quadrupled to $4 trillion within twelve years. And, by early 2009, the public debt had skyrocketed to $11 trillion!

For twenty of the past twenty-eight years, mainstream economists have been shut out of economic policymaking, and conservative politicians have wreaked havoc with the federal budget. Imagine what might have happened if foreign policy had been conducted during that period by politicians without any input from the State Department or Pentagon, and you might be able to grasp the damage done to the economy and the federal budget by politicians during the twelve years of the Reagan-Bush presidencies and again during the eight years under President George W. Bush.

Many economists, including some recipients of the Nobel Prize in the field, did everything within their power to warn the public about impending disaster during the entire period, but the conservative politicians continued their irresponsible fiscal policies anyway.

The deficits during the first six years of Clinton's presidency raised the debt by an additional $1.6 trillion, but it held steady during Clinton's last two years when there were actually small surpluses in the budget. Thus the national debt, that had been just $1 trillion in 1981, was $5.6 trillion when Clinton left office.

The increase in the national debt from just $1 trillion in 1981 to $5.6 trillion just 19 years later was an atrocity against the American people. And it would have cost the nation dearly for decades to come even if the deficit spending had come to a permanent halt in 2000. The interest paid on the national debt for the year, 2000, was an alarming $362 billion. That was almost $1 billion per day! Since there is little likelihood that any of the national debt will ever be repaid, Americans for generations to come will have to continue to pay at least $1 billion per day just for the $5.6 trillion in debt that existed in 2000. The nation should have learned a bitter lesson about what happens when the government cuts taxes without cutting spending. Reaganomics had turned out to be a colossal failure.

During the eight years of the Clinton presidency, competent mainstream professional economists once again played a major role in economic policy making. The Clinton deficit reduction package, which included both spending cuts and tax increases, resulted in a tax structure that was once again capable of generating a balanced budget, or small surpluses, at the full-employment level of output.

During the first six years of the Clinton presidency, the annual budget deficits steadily diminished, as the economy grew and unemployment declined. Finally, in 1999 and 2000, the economy was operating near maximum capacity, and the nation's tax structure was generating enough revenue to eliminate deficits. If the tax structure and spending had continued at 2000 levels, the federal budget would have experienced moderate deficits during the lower stages of the business cycle, when unemployment was rising, and approximately balanced budgets at the peak of the business cycle.

The surpluses of 1999 and 2000 followed 38 consecutive years of budget deficits. It was a time for celebration. The damage done by all those past deficits was in no way undone by the two surplus years. The monstrous deficits from the past were very visible in the form of the $5.6 trillion national debt. But the nation had the opportunity to cap the debt and avoid further deficit spending.

President Clinton's policies had pulled the nation back from the brink that we were so close to when he became President. If his successor had continued to follow sound economic policies the economic outlook would have been reasonably good. But, unfortunately, as was pointed out in detail in Chapter 5, George W. Bush had other plans for America. Some political observers have referred to Bush's first term in office as "Reagan's third term."

Despite the terrible damage done to the economy and the federal budget by twelve years of Reaganomics, George W. Bush picked up right where his father had left off, and led the nation back toward the brink. When we got there, he led us over the edge, taking the whole world with us. Bush was not the only contributor to the economic and financial collapse. Many individuals, government agencies, and business entities were big contributors. But none of them, alone, could have caused, or prevented, the meltdown. However, Bush's policies, actions, and inactions, were a primary cause of the collapse, and he could have prevented it.

On March 20, 2009, the nonpartisan Congressional Budget Office released its analysis of President Barack Obama's ten-year budget proposal. The CBO projected a $1.8 trillion deficit for fiscal year 2009, which ends September 30, 2009, and a $1.4 trillion deficit for fiscal 2010. The Congressional Budget office estimated that, during the period 2010-2019, a total of $9.3 trillion in deficit spending will take place. If the forecast is accurate, it would mean that the national debt would top the $20 trillion mark by 2019! This would be a twentyfold increase in the debt just during the 38-year period of 1981 to 2019.

These numbers are mind boggling, and it is extremely important that the public understand the difference between what is and what could have been. What could have been is a national debt today that was not much higher than the $5.6 trillion debt that existed in 2000. At that time, the nation was experiencing its second straight year without a deficit, and the tax structure was adequate to generate a balanced budget when the economy was operating at full capacity.

During 1999 and 2000, the federal government spent less than it collected in tax revenue, and this feat could have been approximately repeated in

most years. I say "approximately" because automatic spending for some programs, such as unemployment compensation and food stamps, fluctuates
during the various phases of the business cycle.
Likewise, income tax revenue fluctuates with the
business cycle. So, in reality, the government
should aim for small surpluses in some years and
small deficits in other years. If the surpluses approximately offset the deficits, there should be little
increase in the national debt.

The unanticipated spending on war during the
period should have been financed by a temporary
special war tax imposed on the American people
and businesses. This is the way that America has
financed most wars throughout our history. In time
of war, when some Americans are putting their lives
on the line, the rest of the people should also be
asked to make sacrifices in order for the nation to
successfully wage the war without doing significant
damage to the federal budget.

President George W. Bush never called on civilian Americans to make sacrifices during the war
and, instead of raising taxes, he cut them. If the
Bush tax cuts had never been enacted, and if taxes
had been increased by enough to finance the two
wars, it is unlikely that the financial and economic
crises of 2008 would have occurred. But, even if
they had, America would today have the resources
and the capacity to wage an all out war against the
economic and financial forces that threatened the
world.

Because of the policies of the Bush administration, America today finds itself financially disabled
at a time when there is a stronger need than ever for

the United States to take strong and costly actions to help stabilize the world economy.

As far back as the 1980s, I regularly pointed out to my students that the deficits and the growing national debt were handicapping the government and reducing its ability to act decisively in the event of a financial crisis. As the deficits continued and the public debt became larger and larger, I became increasingly worried that, if government economic policies did not change, they would eventually trigger a major financial crisis, and if such a crisis did come, our government would be so weak financially that it would not be able to adequately respond to the crisis. This seems to be the case today.

I'm sure most economists share my outrage when anyone implies that there was no way to see this coming. Economists had plenty of foresight, and we did know that such a day of reckoning was bound to come. That is why we tried so hard to warn the public about the malicious malpractice of our government. Personally, I have spent more than 30 years battling economic illiteracy and promoting economic education. I have tried my best to alert the public to the dangerous economic malpractice that our government was engaging in, but nobody wanted to listen.

Today's economic and financial crises are not like Pearl Harbor or the September 11, 2001 terrorist attacks. Investigations into those cases have revealed that there were hints and tidbits of information that should have been taken more seriously. But there were no outright warnings that officials ignored.

The Wall Street meltdown and the collapse of economies around the world could have been prevented if the warnings of professional economists had been taken more seriously. The four presidents who played a role in the making of today's crises, and most of the members of Congress who supported them, knew that they were placing political considerations above sound economic policy. I believe that historians who carefully study the pathway to the financial fiasco will conclude that Presidents Ronald Reagan, George H.W. Bush, Bill Clinton, and George W. Bush all played a role in the catastrophe.

The American people, who supported the damaging economic policies, could be faulted if they had been capable of understanding what was really going on, but they were not capable. The American education system has failed to educate the American people in the field of economics. We are a nation of economic illiterates with only a small percentage of college graduates having ever taken a course in economics. So we have to place the blame for our economic problems jointly on Wall Street and Washington.

We began this chapter with a quote from Republican Senator Judd Gregg of New Hampshire, who predicted that President Obama's ten-year budget proposal would lead to national bankruptcy. Could such a thing actually happen? Is the United States government now on the verge of national bankruptcy? The answer to this question is both "yes" and "no".

The answer is, no, if we are talking strictly about legal bankruptcy where an entity is taken into court and declared bankrupt. There is no court with the power to declare any nation bankrupt. On the other hand, the dictionary definition of the word, bankrupt, is "Any entity that is unable to pay its debts." The entity may be an individual, a business, or a unit of government. If an individual, a business, or a unit of government is unable to pay its debts, that entity is, by definition, bankrupt.

In this sense, the United States government is not bankrupt yet, but it is dangerously close to bankruptcy. The government has to borrow large sums of money on a regular basis in order to refinance existing debt as well as to cover new deficit spending. If a time were to come when the United States government was unable to pay some of its debt at the time it came due, the government would be bankrupt in terms of the most common meaning of the term. Suppose that foreign investors should panic for some reason and cease buying American debt. That is the kind of financial catastrophe that nobody wants to see. Yet, the deeper we as a nation go into debt, the greater the possibility that this could happen.

In addition to the overwhelming problems of today, the government will face a major additional crisis, beginning in 2017. (The crisis may come much sooner than 2017 if the recession results in big decreases in payroll tax revenue.) Government officials have not yet acknowledged the forthcoming crisis, when Social Security revenue falls below the cost of providing full benefits, and most Americans don't have a clue that such a crisis lies ahead. Nevertheless, it will come as surely as the sun rises each morning.

This problem was thoroughly discussed in Chapter 3, so I will just summarize the details here. The Social Security Amendments of 1983 included large increases in payroll taxes in order to build up a large reserve in the trust fund for paying full Social Security benefits to the baby boom generation. Taxes were raised high enough so that the baby boomers paid the full cost of benefits for the generation that preceded them, which was customary, and prepaid most of the cost of their own benefits, which was not customary.

That hefty increase in payroll taxes has been generating more revenue than is needed to pay current benefits since 1985, and it would have continued to generate surpluses until 2017, if the economy had continued to prosper. However, the surpluses will end in 2017 (or perhaps much sooner if the recession remains severe for very long.), and Social Security will experience growing annual deficits after that.

This means that the government will need additional funds in order to pay full Social Security benefits, once the payroll tax revenue falls below the cost of paying benefits. The plan was for the surpluses that came in between 1985 and 2017 to be saved and invested in order to build up a huge reserve in the trust fund. Then, during the years 2018 to 2041, the government would gradually draw enough out of the reserve, year after year, to supplement the inadequate payroll tax revenue. By 2017, the increased Social Security taxes should have generated enough revenue so that the trust fund should hold approximately $3.7 trillion in reserves. This would enable the government to pay full benefits until 2041.

Unfortunately, the government did not save and invest the surplus Social Security money. Instead, it used the surplus like a giant slush fund, and spent every penny of it on other programs. Most people believe that the surplus money was invested in good-as-gold public-issue U.S. Treasury bonds, but it was not. It was borrowed by the government and spent. Once money is spent, there is nothing left to invest.

According to the Social Security administration, at the end of 2008, the trust fund held $2.4 trillion in assets. It makes a lot of difference to a lot of people as to whether or not that $2.4 trillion in assets is real. If it is not real, then, as bleak as the financial outlook of our government already seems today, it is $2.4 trillion worse off than we are being told. This money is supposed to be used to supplement the inadequate payroll tax revenue during the deficit years of 2017 to 2041. Without the money, the government cannot pay full Social Security benefits once the payroll tax revenue falls below the cost of benefits.

Although the government has already spent the money, it is legally and ethically obligated to repay the Social Security trust fund every dollar that it has "borrowed." But, is the government financially able to repay the money? Where will the government find that much money, given the current financial crisis? It could raise taxes if that were politically feasible. But how many members of Congress are going to have the political fortitude to vote for increased taxes in order to replace previous tax revenue that was "borrowed" and spent by the government for purposes other than that for which it was collected?

The American people have already paid that $2.4 trillion in payroll taxes for purposes of building up the trust fund. To tell the public, "We're sorry, but we spent that money for something else, so we need to tax you again," would not be an easy sell.

If it is not politically feasible to raise taxes, what other options does the government have for raising the money? They could consider borrowing it, but there is a limit to how much even the United States government can borrow, even if government officials do not recognize or acknowledge this fact.

It may come as a surprise (maybe even a shock) to some readers, but our biggest foreign creditor is China. Yes, communist China, the country that some people fear might be our greatest enemy. The American government owes approximately $1 trillion to China. Even worse, the United States government is counting on China to lend us a lot more money to help us get out of the financial pinch we have gotten ourselves into.

On Friday, March 13, 2009, at a news conference, China's Premier Wen Jiabao issued a stern warning to the United States about the nation's current financial condition. Wen said, "Of course we are concerned about the safety of our assets. To be honest I'm a little bit worried. I would like to call on the United States to honor its words, stay a credible nation, and ensure the safety of Chinese assets."

Analysts estimate that China currently keeps approximately half of its $2 trillion in foreign currency reserves in U.S. Treasuries. One of the first foreign nations visited by Secretary of State, Hillary Clinton, was China, and Clinton's primary mission was to reassure the Chinese government about United States finances and to encourage China to keep the money coming.

It seems to me that owing so much money to China is a national security issue. It is hard to get tough with your banker, and it seems that our large debt to China gives them a great deal of political leverage. If the Chinese were to suddenly decide to withdraw the $1 trillion they now have invested in U.S. Treasuries and invest it elsewhere, it would result in higher interest rates and a drop in the value of the dollar in international markets. It could even set off a panic, causing other nations to stop buying our debt, thus driving the value of the dollar still lower.

Given the issues discussed above, I don't think that borrowing money from foreign lenders to repay the $2.4 trillion that the government has "borrowed" from the trust fund and spent for non-Social Security purposes seems very feasible. Of course, they wouldn't have to borrow all the money at once. They could just borrow the money needed to pay full benefits on a year by year basis.

But, as the years go by, the amount of money that would need to be borrowed, gets larger and larger. According to the 2008 Social Security Trustees Report (Table VI.F9), in order to pay full benefits in 2020, the government would have to come up with $107 billion to add to the inadequate payroll tax revenue. In 2025, paying full benefits would require the government to come up with $275 billion, and for 2030, there would be a need for $471 billion. In 2035, the shortfall is $656 billion, and in 2040 the government would have to add $808 billion to the payroll tax revenue in order to pay full Social Security benefits.

It will not be easy for the government to repay the borrowed Social Security money, either through higher taxes or with borrowed funds, given all the other financial demands resulting from the financial crisis. If the government is unable to repay the borrowed money, the only other option is for the government to default on its debt to Social Security and cut benefits.

For years, I have suggested that the government might actually default on its debt to Social Security, and the likelihood of that happening is higher today than ever before. I am well aware that most economists and other financial experts have long argued that the federal government could never default on any of its debt because of the catastrophic effect that such action would have on world financial markets. I agree that the government cannot, and will not, ever default on any of its public issue Treasury bills, notes and bonds. These instruments are as good as gold, and they are default proof.

Unfortunately, however, none of the Social Security surplus funds were invested in such instruments. Actually, none of the surplus Social Security funds were invested in anything. The money was all spent. The confusion comes from the myth that the Social Security trust fund holds $2.4 trillion worth of United States Government Treasury bonds.

As was made clear in a statement by David Walker, Comptroller General of the Government Accountability Office (GAO), on January 21, 2005, "There are no stocks or bonds or real estate in the trust fund. It holds nothing of real value to draw down."

The trust fund holds only government IOUs which serve as an accounting record of how much Social Security money has been borrowed and spent by the government. These IOUs are called "special issues of the Treasury." They are held only by the trust funds and are non-marketable. They cannot be bought or sold at any price, and thus they have no market value.

The government could default on these special Social Security IOUs without defaulting on any of its other debt. Other nations might frown on such action by our government, but, since they would not be directly affected, I think other countries would view such action as an internal matter between the United States Government and its citizens. As long as the United States Government continues to honor all public-issue Treasuries, I don't think failure to repay its debt to Social Security would have any significant international ramifications.

Those who say the government can never default on any of its debt are wrong. The government can, and very well may, default on its debt to the Social Security trust fund, citing the world financial collapse, or government insolvency, as the reason for their action. I think defaulting on its debt to Social Security would be a terrible thing for the United States Government to do to the American people. However, the government clearly has the legal authority to default if it chooses to do so.

The United States government has accumulated so much debt that the nation's capacity to deal with problems, both domestic and international, has been greatly diminished. This is especially true because so much of the public debt is owed to foreign investors.

During the early years of my teaching career, I was able to truthfully tell college students that the national debt was no big deal, and that interest payments on the debt went right back into the American economy. That was true because almost all of the national debt was a debt that "we" the people of the United States owed to "us" the people of the United States. The nation, as a whole, was neither richer nor poorer because of the debt.

That situation has changed dramatically over the years as the nation's runaway deficits have gotten bigger and bigger. The money that American investors are willing to invest in United States Treasury Bonds is not nearly enough to satisfy the government's growing appetite for borrowed funds. The net result is that, as of March 2009, approximately 28 percent of the total debt, and nearly 45 percent of the publicly held debt, was owed to foreigners. This means that, when the United States government makes interest payments on the debt held by foreigners, valuable resources flow out of the country to the outside world.

As mentioned above, the country that we owe the most foreign debt to is Mainland China, and Japan is the second largest foreign lender to the United States. However, since the government borrows money by offering United States Treasuries at auction in the open market, we owe at least some debt to many other foreign countries, including Russia, The United Kingdom, Brazil, Germany, Switzerland, Mexico, India, Norway, and France.

The total interest cost of the national debt for 2008 was $451 billion. At least $125 billion of that was paid to foreign investors. As any debtor knows, it is extremely painful to pay interest on debt. It seems like money down the drain because it does not reduce the debt at all. Imagine how much that $451 billion could have bought in the form of education, health care, road construction, or even tax relief. The interest cost for 2008 was slightly more than the combined federal government spending on health ($280.6 billion), education ($89.1 billion), and transportation,($77.7 billion).

Interest rates are very low today, by historical standards, but they will not always be low. When interest rates rise, the amount of interest cost on the same amount of debt will be higher. For example, if current interest rates were to double over a period of time, the $451 billion interest cost would double to $902 billion.

The United States government has dug itself into a very deep hole over the past 28 years. We are in so deep that we can barely see the dim light at the top of the hole. Unfortunately, instead of filling the hole in, our government is digging it deeper and deeper!

CHAPTER EIGHT

Countdown to Financial Meltdown

People around the world are shocked and confused as a result of the financial and economic crises which have brought so much suffering. They cannot begin to comprehend how the world financial system and the economies of almost all nations could have deteriorated so much so fast. Prior to 2008, there was little indication to the average person that anything was wrong with the financial system, so how could things have changed so much in such a short period of time?

Some economists had been warning about irresponsible government policies for years, and, at least a few of them, warned that, if we continued with the reckless policies, a day of reckoning would eventually come. But I don't think many economists thought it would come so soon or be so severe.

With the benefit of hindsight, we can go back and see that there were at least a few hints of trouble more than a year before the actual Wall Street meltdown. On July 19, 2007, Federal Reserve Chairman, Ben Bernanke, told the United States

Senate Banking Committee that there might be as much as $100 billion in losses associated with subprime mortgages. This may have raised some concerns in the minds of members of Congress, but average citizens never knew about the warning. On August 22, 2007, Countrywide Financial Corporation, the biggest U.S. mortgage lender, sold $2 billion of preferred stock to Bank of America in order to bolster its finances. This raised a lot of eyebrows in the financial industry, and some began to wonder if any other large financial institutions were in trouble. The anxiety in the banking community was greatly heightened when on January 11, 2008, Bank of America agreed to buy Countrywide for approximately $4 billion.

A month later, it became clear that Countrywide was not just an isolated case when Bear Stearns became insolvent and was purchased by JP Morgan Chase for 7 percent of its market value in a sale brokered by the Fed and the U.S. Treasury Department. Just 4 months later, IndyMac Bancorp, Inc., the second-biggest independent U.S. mortgage lender, was seized by federal regulators after a run by depositors depleted its cash.

On September 7, 2008 the U.S. government seized control of Fannie Mae and Freddie Mac, the largest U.S. mortgage-finance companies. On September 15, Lehman Brothers Holdings, Inc. filed the largest bankruptcy in history, and on the same day, Bank of America agreed to acquire Merrill Lynch for about $50 billion. The following day, September 16, American International Group, Inc. (AIG) accepted an $85 billion loan from the Federal Reserve to avert the worst financial collapse in history, and the government took over the company.

As one bank after another failed in the United States in mid-September 2008, banks in other countries, around the world, were also failing. The world's financial system was collapsing, and there was little anyone could do to halt the momentum. The unthinkable was happening.

On September 21, 2008 Goldman Sachs Group and Morgan Stanley received approval to become commercial banks regulated by the Fed in order to widen their sources of funding. On September 26, Washington Mutual, Inc. was seized by federal regulators and its assets were sold to JPMorgan Chase. This was the biggest United States bank failure in history.

During September, October, and November, 2008, there was so much bad economic news, that even the most vocal Pollyanna's were having trouble seeing a silver lining in the dark cloud that had descended upon the world. As the election passed and President Barack Obama was inaugurated on January 20, the mood throughout America was very different from what it would have been in the absence of the avalanche of bad economic news.

Although much of the financial system collapse occurred over a relatively short period of time, the factors that led to the collapse had been years in the making. Many economists believe that one of the biggest factors in the collapse was the deregulation of banks which resulted from the enactment of the Gramm-Leach-Bliley Act in 1999.

This law repealed part of the 1933 Glass-Steagall Act, which was passed during the Great

Depression in an effort to prevent a repeat of the banking crisis of the 1930s. The Glass Steagall Act had placed strict regulations on the banking industry, and some argued that removing those regulations was very risky. North Dakota Senator Byron Dorgan warned at the time, "I think we will look back in 10 years' time and say we should not have done this, but we did because we forgot the lessons of the past."

The Gramm-Leach-Bliley Act was signed into law by President Bill Clinton on November 12, 1999. The final version of the bill was passed by the Senate 90-8 and by the House 362-57. Although the legislation was sponsored by the Republicans, and initially received stiff opposition from Congressional Democrats, the final version was overwhelmingly supported by both parties. Therefore, if this legislation was one of the primary causes of the Wall Street meltdown, members of Congress from both parties, and Democratic President Bill Clinton all share the blame.

The triggering mechanism for the ultimate financial collapse was the subprime mortgage crisis. In order to understand how this unfolded, it is necessary first to talk about how home mortgage loans were tranformed into mortgage-backed securites by Wall Street investment firms.

Historically, banks would make mortgage loans only to people who had a substantial down payment, a good credit record, and adequate income to repay the loan. There was little risk to the banks in making such loans. Most people would repay the loans as scheduled and, if a few people defaulted, the bank would simply foreclose on the property and sell it for at least enough to pay off the loan balance. When a bank loaned a maximum of 80 percent of the appraised value of a home, and home values were either stable or rising, there was little likelihood that the bank could loose any money even if the borrower defaulted.

The safety and good yields on mortgages made it attractive for Wall Street investment firms to buy large numbers of mortgages, bundle them together in large packages, and then sell shares of the mort-gage backed securities to investors. Demand for these mortgage backed securities became so high in the early 2000s that banks sought to make more and more mortgage loans so they could sell them to the Wall Street investment firms at a good profit. At one point in 2003, the demand was so high that eve-ryone who met the qualifications for a conventional mortgage loan was able to get one. But, even then, the demand for mortgage-backed securities was not met. It was at this point that the seeds of the 2008 meltdown began to be sowed. And it was at this time that adequate government regulations could have prevented the misery that the whole world now finds itself in.

Since everyone who met the qualifications for mortgage loans were able to get such loans, the only way to make more mortgage loans was to lower the mortgage qualification requirements so that more people would qualify for such loans. These circum-stances gave birth to the subprime mortgage loan. Subprime mortgage loans are made to people who do not qualify for the standard conventional mort-gage that usually required a 20 percent down pay-ment, a good credit history, and a good income. By there very nature, subprime mortgage loans are more risky than conventional mortgage loans, so the interest rate is higher for such loans.

The first subprime loans called SIVA loans required borrowers only to "state" their income—not prove it. However, the borrower did have to verify that they had money in the bank. The next modification in loan qualifications resulted in NIVA loans which meant that borrowers still had to verify assets but didn't even have to "state" their incomes. With these loans, the lender was no longer interested in what the borrower did for a living or how much he or she earned. These relaxed rules made a lot more people eligible for mortgage loans, but even they did not satisfy the huge appetite of global investors who wanted to invest in mortgage backed securities.

Finally, the eligibility requirements were almost eliminated, and people were able to get no income, no asset verification (NINA) mortgage loans. All you needed was to have a credit score to get a NINA loan. You didn't have to have any income or any assets. Also, you did not have to have a good credit score. You just had to have a score above a minimal level set by the lenders.

By 2006, more than 20 percent of all mortgage loans in the United States were subprime. The banks and mortgage companies sought borrowers from middle-class families who had accumulated too much debt to qualify for a conventional mortgage loan as well as low-income families who were seeking their share of the American dream through home ownership. In 2007, 11 percent of all subprime loans were made to first-time home buyers. The other 89 percent went to borrowers who chose to refinance their homes in order to get some additional equity out with which to pay off credit card debt, pay for health care, or meet other needs.

Many of the subprime loans were made at relatively low interest rates (often called "teaser" rates) for the first two or three years. However, the rates were adjustable, and when it came time to reset them, they usually went up substantially, causing monthly payments for many buyers to rise so high that they could no longer make those payments. This is when foreclosure rates began to soar. Apparently many realtors and lenders used the hard-sell approach to encourage people to buy homes that they could not afford. With little or no down payment, and artificially low interest rates initially, a lot of people were fooled into believing they could afford unaffordable homes. When the interest rates were reset and the borrowers discovered that they were in over their heads, many simply walked away and allowed the mortgage owners to foreclose on them.

The housing bubble masked the subprime problem as long as prices continued to rise. Up until 2006, the housing market was booming. It was easy to get loans, so a lot of people bought homes. This increased demand caused housing prices to increase. These rising prices attracted speculative buyers who hoped to buy homes, keep them for a short period, and then sell them at a profit. The speculative demand, added to the demand of those who were obtaining easy loans and buying homes to live in, sent home prices even higher.

Because of the rising prices, the ultimate consequences of the "bad" loans was delayed. As a result of the easy lending practices, and the rising value of homes, people who had trouble making payments just took out second loans to make ends meet. But the belief that housing prices would continue to rise indefinitely was based on wishful thinking, not solid economics. Prices finally rose so high that families found homes no longer affordable.

A chain of interactions, similar to those of the housing bubble, but in the opposite direction, began to appear. Default rates and foreclosures escalated. This put even more empty homes on the market. With the oversupply of houses and the lack of demand, home prices began to drop. As panic began to set in, prices plummeted lower and lower. In late 2006 and early 2007 home prices took a real nosedive, and that is when Wall Street began to panic.

Why were banks willing to issue such risky loans? In the past, banks were very careful when making mortgage loans, especially those local banks that held the loans on their books until the loan was totally repaid. Many small community banks have rarely sold mortgages to outside investors. They focus on doing business with local customers who deposit money in the banks and borrow money from the banks. When they make a 20-year mortgage loan to a local resident, they want to make absolutely sure that the borrower will be able to repay the loan. That is why a sizeable down payment and proof of sufficient income to repay the loan, are required. Such banks would be irresponsible if they used depositors' money to make risky loans. It is because of such sound lending practices that there were almost no bank failures from the enactment of

FDIC during the Great Depression until very recent years.

That all changed with the deregulation of the banking industry, beginning with the repeal of the Glass-Steagall Act in 1999. With the rules relaxed, many of the banks that issued mortgage loans did not keep them. They almost immediately sold the mortgages to Wall Street investment firms. Since the banks did not keep the mortgages, they didn't have to concern themselves with whether or not the loans would ever be repaid. They made their money upfront by making the loans and then selling the mortgages. No matter how risky a loan was over the long run, there was little risk to the bank that made the loan and then promptly sold the mortgage.

Wall Street firms had been packaging bundles of mortgages, and selling shares to investors for many years, with no major problems. Credit rating agencies like Standard and Poor's and Moody's had usually given the mortgage-backed securities the top AAA rating, the same as they gave to United States government bonds. The problem came when these mortgage bundles began to include a few subprime mortgages, along with the conventional mortgages. Nobody seemed to notice at first, and gradually more and more subprime mortgages were included in the packages. However, once the default and foreclosure rates began to build up momentum, investors started to discover that they had "toxic" assets on their books.

It is important to note that the subprime mortgage crisis was only the mechanism that triggered the financial meltdown. It was not sufficient, in and of itself, to bring down the whole financial system. It was essentially just the first domino to fall. Irresponsible behavior on the part of the government, businesses, and consumers had made the whole system vulnerable. Consumers had been living beyond their means for years, just like the government, and corporate mismanagement had put many businesses on very shaky financial ground. Once the meltdown had been triggered, the panic and plummeting confidence of both consumers and investors kept it going.

The recession was already underway even before the financial meltdown, having started in December 2007, but the meltdown made the recession much more severe. As consumers reduced their spending, employers laid off workers. As more layoffs took place, consumer spending contracted still more. This vicious cycle of, consumers not buying because they don't have jobs, and, employers not hiring because consumers are not buying what they produce, is what caused the economy to hit rock bottom in the 1930s and stay there for an entire decade.

The reason that the Great Depression was so deep and lasted for so long, is that the economic system broke down and, without appropriate actions by the government to fix it, the economy stayed broken. Roosevelt's public works projects helped the economy a great deal by creating jobs and generating paychecks that would be spent and create still more jobs. However, the government and the American people were not willing to provide strong enough medicine to bring the economy totally out of the depression. Although there was substantial improvement in the economy, there were indications, during the years immediately preceding the attack on Pearl Harbor and America's entry into World War II , that the economy might be slipping back into depression.

However, the enormous spending that resulted from the war finally provided enough aggregate demand to pull the economy out of the depression. It is extremely important that we understand clearly that World War II did not rescue America from the Great Depression. It was the spending on the war, not the war itself, that ended the Great Depression. If the United States had been willing to spend as much on domestic projects, like building schools, libraries and roads, as was spent on the war, the depression could have ended, and prosperity could have been restored to the nation, without a single bullet being fired.

Once the economy broke down, it would have remained broken down indefinitely without a government rescue. The factories would have continued to set idle because nobody was buying the products that the factories made. Consumers, who very much wanted to buy products, were unable to do so because they had lost their jobs and had no source of income. The public was consumed by fear. People tried to hoard whatever small amount of money they had because they were afraid there would be an even greater need for it in the future.

The state of the economy today is similar to what it was in the early days of the Great Depression. Consumer spending is way down, and each month brings a new round of layoffs. As more and more workers lose their jobs, consumer spending is further reduced. And, as consumer spending is reduced, even more workers are laid off. Thus, the recession is getting deeper and deeper, and nobody knows, for sure, when the economy will hit bottom

In April 2009, the International Monetary Fund (IMF), which represents 185 member countries, predicted that unemployment levels would continue to rise through 2010, and, once a recovery begins, the IMF expects it to be "sluggish relative to past recoveries." Also in April, Paul Volker, former Fed chairman and a senior economic adviser to President Obama, expressed a similarly pessimistic view of the economy during a speech at Vanderbilt University. He said, the financial system "is not quite comatose, but it's on life support." With regard to the economy, Volker said, "None of us has seen a decline in economic activity at the rate of speed seen last year." He pointed out that troubles in the financial system continue to plague the economy, and vice versa.

In summary, the multitude of problems, that led to the financial meltdown and the severe recession, have been accumulating for nearly three decades. The United States government and the American people have been living beyond their means during the entire period. The huge tax cuts, that were not matched by corresponding spending cuts, under both President Ronald Reagan and President George W. Bush, contributed heavily to the $11 trillion national debt that exists today. A similar build up in consumer debt during the same period made consumers extremely vulnerable to any financial crisis.

The repeal of the Glass-Steagall Act in 1999 sealed the economic fate of the nation and the world. This inexcusably, irresponsible act by our government doomed us to repeat history because it activated a time bomb that would continue to tick until it exploded. Senator Dorgan's warning that we would look back in 10 years' time and say "we should not have done this," was right on target.

The Glass-Steagall Act, enacted during the Great Depression for the explicit purpose of preventing financial institutions from engaging in reckless behavior that could lead to another financial meltdown, had served the nation well for decades. However, after years of lobbying, which included the spending of billions of dollars, the financial industry managed to free itself from the protective constraints of the law by getting it repealed.

What did the financial industry get for all that money it paid to politicians? It got a few years to wallow in greed. Since the cat was taken away, the Wall Street mice were free to play, but the party was short-lived. When the time bomb went off in 2008, the Wall Street mice were the first to feel the blast, but soon the whole financial world would come tumbling down.

The immeasurable cost of this financial fiasco, in terms of both dollars and human suffering, cannot even be estimated for years, or perhaps even decades. In financial terms, I believe the nation and the world are in one of the most dangerous periods of all history. We can compare the current situation with that of the 1930s, but when we do, we must remember that we are comparing apples to oranges. We live in a very different world today than that of the 1930s. Our nation was not at war during the time of the Great Depression. We were able to devote all our resources to battling the economic problems. By contrast, today the nation's resources have been severely depleted by two ongoing wars.

In the 1930s, the national debt was small and not a major burden to the nation. Today, we are reaping the harvest of nearly three decades of reckless fiscal policy, and we are on the verge of national bankruptcy with a public debt of $11 trillion. That debt is growing so fast that the nation will accumulate more debt in the next twelve months than was accumulated during the first 200 years of our history. Yet, we are in need of massive resources with which to battle the financial and economic crises. Where will we get the needed resources? Can we count on China and other foreign investors to finance our bailout efforts?

CHAPTER NINE

A Voice Crying in the Wilderness

As stated in the preface, I appeared on CNN with Lou Waters to discuss my book, *The Alleged Budget Surplus, Social Security, & Voodoo Economics* on September 27, 2000. When I tried to explain that there was really no significant budget surplus, except for the Social Security surplus, and told Waters that the government was using Social Security money for other programs, he looked at me in disbelief.

> "We're not hearing any of this in the news," Waters said. "I'm involved in the news. Are you a voice crying in the wilderness? And if not, why haven't we seen a presidential candidate, any presidential candidate, talk about this?"

I was a voice crying in the wilderness in September 2000, and I have continued to be such a voice ever since. I have tried my best to alert the American public to the ongoing raiding of the Social Security trust fund and the runaway budget deficits, but almost nobody wants to listen.

Actually, I have been a voice crying in the wilderness for more than three decades. After completing my Ph.D. in Economics at Indiana University in 1970, I began teaching economics to college students at Eastern Illinois University. That is when I first became aware of just how economically illiterate the American population is. I saw it in my students, in the community, and even among my teaching colleagues in other academic fields. Basic economic principles, that one has to understand in order to make any sense out of the economic proposals being put forth by political leaders, were either poorly understood, or not understood at all, by anyone except trained economists.

I saw this as a major failure of the American education system. My children attended what was otherwise a very good high school in the University town. But, to my astonishment, the local high school did not offer even an elective course in economics. I was told that the primary reason they didn't offer economics was that none of the teachers wanted to teach the subject because none of them had received any training in the field.

Of course, the school taught chemistry, physics, calculus, astronomy, foreign languages, and just about every other course that one would expect to see offered by a high-quality high school. The only gap in their curriculum that I was aware of was economics, a subject that would affect the lives and livelihoods of students almost more than any other subject that the school taught.

I was also disappointed in how few college students were required to take a course in economics. Only certain majors required the study of economics. Most students could become a college graduate without ever coming face to face with the subject of economics. Not only that, but most of my colleagues, in other departments, had been able to obtain a Ph.D. degree in their field without ever being exposed to economics.

I couldn't understand why a course in economics was not a general education requirement that every college graduate would have to take. How could we consider anyone well-educated who had no idea of what causes unemployment or inflation, and didn't know the difference between a budget deficit and the national debt?

It was in 1975, that I resolved to dedicate my career as an economist to the cause of reducing economic illiteracy and promoting economic education. I began by writing the book, *Understanding Inflation and Unemployment,* which became an alternate selection of *Fortune Book Club* when it was published in 1976. This was a time when the United States was experiencing a combination of both high unemployment and high inflation. Historically, there had been a tradeoff relationship between inflation and unemployment such that a country usually did not have to deal with high levels of both at the same time. My book represented an effort to explain the special circumstances that had led to the inflation-unemployment problems of the 1970s.

In 1986, Random House published my high school economics textbook, *Understanding Economics,* which was used in more than 600 schools nationwide. I felt good about the contribution the book was making toward reducing economic illiteracy at the high school level but, of course, it couldn't do any good in high schools that continued to refuse to offer their students the opportunity to study economics.

In 1996, the first edition of my book, *Demystifying Economics: The Book That Makes Economics Accessible to Everyone,* was published. A second edition was published in 2000, and an expanded third edition was published in 2008. That book is designed to make economics accessible to people who have never had any formal training in the subject, and I think it has been successful in that regard. In the words of the *Louisville Courier-Journal,*

"...Smith provides an easily understood layman's approach to the perceived mysteries of economics. The book has the potential to be a serious weapon in the battle against economic illiteracy...I believe that readers of *Demystifying Economics* will learn both what economics is and how it can contribute to their understanding of the world."

In 1990, I began writing a weekly self-syndicated newspaper column on the economy called, "Economic Alert." I felt that somebody had to do something to educate the public, so I began warning my readers about the disastrous economic path the nation was following.

My column, which appeared in 30 newspapers, soon became very controversial, and I got many hostile letters from Bush supporters. I was labeled a "Bush Basher," and was called "un-American," a "Marxist" and numerous other choice names. Letters to the editor of newspapers that carried my column urged the newspapers to stop running the column, and some did. I was amazed at the hostility that came my way simply because I was pointing out the flaws of Reaganomics and warning that a day of reckoning would eventually come if we didn't change course.

As the economic malpractice continued undeterred, I felt compelled to do more than just write about the problem. I drafted a proposal for the creation of a National Economic Advisory Council that would serve as a watchdog for the American people to ensure that sound economic policies were followed. I took the proposal to my congressman and urged him to introduce legislation for the creation of such a council. I expressed a desire for him to communicate the proposal to Senator Daniel Moynihan to see if he might be interested in sponsoring such legislation in the Senate.

Congressman Bruce talked about the proposal on the floor of the House, and it was inserted into the Congressional Record. A portion of page E2561 of the July 31, 1990 Congressional Record, which includes my proposal, is reproduced below.

HON. TERRY L. BRUCE
OF ILLINOIS
IN THE HOUSE OF REPRESENTATIVES
Tuesday July 31, 1990

Mr. BRUCE: Mr. Speaker, Dr. Allen Smith of Eastern Illinois University in Charleston, IL, has written an excellent column proposing a national economic advisory council. I ask that it be put in the CONGRESSIONAL RECORD, and I urge my colleagues to give it careful consideration. His message is something all of us should ponder.

UNDERSTANDING ECONOMICS No. 28
(By Allen Smith)
THE NEED FOR A NATIONAL
ECONOMIC ADVISORY COUNCIL

In an effort to get the economy out of its current mess and prevent economic malpractice in the future, I propose the creation of a nonpartisan national economic advisory council made up of nine of the best economists in America. The council members, who would serve nine-year staggered terms, would be appointed by the President and confirmed by Congress.

Council members would be ineligible for reappointment so they could remain independent of partisan politics. Since it is essential that council members have a strong grasp of basic economics, only professionally trained economists would be eligible to serve on the council. The council would have only advisory powers, but it would be mandated by law to issue periodic public reports on the state of the economy and on economic policy.

The purpose of such a council would be to serve as a watchdog for the American people to ensure that sound economic policies are followed. Sound economic policy is Republican, Democratic, conservative, or liberal policy. It is policy based on basic economic principles which are supported by the majority of professionally trained economists. Like members of any other profession, economists disagree on certain aspects of economic policy, however there are many fundamental principles of economics upon which most economists agree. It is some of these most basic fundamental principles that have been ignored in recent years.

This proposal will be about as popular with most politicians as a bad toothache. But if enough Americans supported such a proposal it could be enacted into law. Since members of the council would be appointed, and ineligible for reappointment, they could put the interest of the economy and the American people ahead of any partisan political goals. They would be free to openly disagree with the President and Congress, and they would be obligated to report economic malpractice to the public.

Since the council would have only advisory powers, it could not prevent all economic malpractice or ensure sound economic policy at all times. But, since it would be free to criticize government economic policies without fear of reprisals, it would tend to force the government to pursue responsible economic policies. It would also ensure that professional economists have advisory input into national economic policy.

The actual structure and functioning of any such economic advisory council could differ substantially from my proposal. The important thing is that the American people need a group of highly competent economists who are looking out for the public interests instead of the interests of partisan politicians. Such a council would also benefit the many government officials who have had little or no formal training in the subject of economics. These officials cannot formulate sound economic policies without the advice of competent economists.

Since members of the President's Council of Economic Advisers are selected on the basis of their compatibility with the President's political goals, they serve the political interests of the President which are not always compatible with sound economic policies.   The American people need a council of nonpartisan competent professional economists who are mandated by law to promote economic policies that will best serve the long-term interests of the American economy and the American people.

I have already met privately with a member of the U.S. Congress to discuss the feasibility of creating such a council. He is testing reaction to the proposal in Washington, and he may draft a bill proposing legislation that would create such a council.   Enacting such legislation will require massive support from the general public. Politicians will not take the initiative in creating a council that would serve as a watchdog for the American people to ensure that politicians put the interests of the American economy above their own political interests. Such legislation will be possible only if the American people demand it.   If you support the creation of a nonpartisan national economic advisory council, please send copies of this column, along with your letters of support, to your elected representatives in Washington. We must do more than talk about the need for sound economic policies. We must take action to ensure that they become a reality. Our future, and the future of our children and grandchildren is at stake.

I am even more convinced today than I was in 1990 that the American people need some kind of independent council of competent economists to monitor economic policies and blow the whistle on politicians who put personal political interests above the interests of the economy and the American people. The specific provisions of the proposal could be altered in various ways and still serve the same purpose. The important thing is to have competent economists monitoring economic policies and reporting economic malpractice to the public at large. If such a council had existed during the past decade, I don't believe there would have been a financial meltdown.

I began doing research on the federal budget in late 1999. That research led to the publication of my book, *The Alleged Budget Surplus, Social Security, and Voodoo Economics,* in 2000. It was while doing research for this book that I made an unexpected, and very troubling, discovery. I discovered the ongoing fraudulent government practice of spending the Social Security surplus revenue on other government programs. At first, I couldn't believe my findings. The elected officials of the United States government surely would not spend the Social Security contributions of American workers on other government programs without either the knowledge or permission of those workers. But, the more I researched the subject, the clearer it became that the government had done, and was continuing to do, exactly that.

I was outraged, and I wanted to tell the whole world so they would be outraged too. But nobody wanted to listen. It just didn't seem credible that our own government, both Democrats and Republicans, would engage in such fraud against the American people.

As part of my efforts to alert the public, I began sending material to candidate Al Gore in early 2000. I sent him advance copies of my book, research findings, and several letters. I urged Gore to put distance between himself and Clinton on Social Security and take a stand against the continued use of Social Security money for non-Social Security purposes. I used multiple channels of communication in sending the material to Gore in order to be sure that at least some of it got to him.

I cannot be sure that I was the source of Gore's idea to propose the Social Security lockbox, and to make the raiding of the trust fund a major campaign issue. However, the important point is that Gore did take a stand against the continued raiding of the trust fund, which resulted in George W. Bush taking a similar stand. Thus, during the 2000 campaign, both Gore and Bush entered into a new covenant with the American people on how Social Security revenue would be treated in the future. They both acknowledged that the trust fund had been raided in the past and pledged to end the raiding.

With both candidates making such a pledge, it appeared that no matter who won the 2000 election, the days of using Social Security money for non-Social Security purposes were over. But that was not the case. We will never know whether or not Al Gore would have honored his promise to protect

Social Security if he had become president. But we do know that George W. Bush did not honor his promise. He continued to raid the Social Security trust fund just like his father, Ronald Reagan, and Bill Clinton had been doing for years.

I tried very hard to get the Social Security fraud recognized and reported by the media, but my success was very limited. I had the good fortune of being one of two guests to appear on CNBC on February 26, 2004, the morning after Greenspan's first assault on Social Security was launched. And I used the opportunity to say, "Alan Greenspan should be ashamed of himself for what he is not telling the American people!" I also had the opportunity to discuss my views on CNNfn and more than 150 live radio talk shows, but still the public would not buy the notion that Bush was spending the Social Security surplus.

The media and the public just would not even entertain the notion that what I was saying could possibly be true. Trying to convince them that Bush was spending every dollar of the Social Security surplus, in violation of both federal law and his promise to the American people, was like trying to convince them that I had taken a ride in a UFO. My suggestions were just rejected out of hand, and no major newspaper would even consider publishing the numerous op-ed articles I submitted.

Once George W. Bush was inaugurated, it became clear that he planned to abandon the economic policies of Bill Clinton and return the nation to the policies of his father and Ronald Reagan, the same policies that had already inflicted so much damage on America. It was unthinkable that the American people would allow this to happen.

Although my efforts, and the efforts of many other economists, to alert the public to the dangers of Reaganomics, had failed repeatedly to have any impact, I felt that I had to try to abort another round of Reaganomics. After all, Bush could not make radical changes without the support of the United States Congress. So I decided to try to make my case to the United States Senate.

On February 12, 2001, less than a month into the George W. Bush presidency, I mailed a package, via Priority Mail, to each and every one of the 100 United States Senators. The package included a copy of my book, *"The Alleged Budget Surplus, Social Security, and Voodoo Economics,"* a video of my CNN interview with Lou Waters, and a very long letter. In the letter, I pleaded with the senators to block Bush's new program. Below is a copy of the letter I sent to Democratic senators. I also sent a similar letter to all Republican senators.

February 12, 2001

The Honorable Chris Dodd
448 Russell Senate Office Building
The United States Senate
Washington, D.C. 20510

Dear Senator Dodd,

I am alarmed by the possibility that this nation could return to another round of Reaganomics, with all the adverse consequences we suffered the first time around, by enacting President Bush's proposed massive tax cut.

I have been battling economic illiteracy in America ever since my first book, *Understanding Inflation and Unemployment* was published in 1976. Today, five books and 25 years later, economic illiteracy is a greater threat to us than ever before. I published two new books last year—*Demystifying Economics* in April, and *The Alleged Budget Surplus, Social Security, & Voodoo Economics* in September—and I have been doing everything in my power to wake up the public to the danger that economic illiteracy poses for America...

...I have been following the economy and the federal budget closely for the past 25 years, and I wrote a syndicated newspaper column on the economy during the early 1990s. I watched in disbelief when the Congress enacted the Reagan economic proposals, knowing that there was almost an absolute certainty that they would lead to gigantic deficits, skyrocketing growth in the national debt, and severe damage to the U.S. economy, as they did. I am both alarmed and dumbfounded that the nation is about to follow another economically illiterate president down the same road, and I want to do everything in my power to prevent this from happening.

I believe that the Democratic party is missing a golden opportunity to educate voters on the terrible results of Reaganomics, and portray themselves as the "guardians of the American economy" by opposing President Bush's irresponsible and reckless economic proposals. I have not heard anyone even mention the catastrophic effect of Reaganomics on working Americans in terms of massive layoffs and record unemployment rates...

...I would strongly urge the Democratic Party to put forth an alternative economic package that includes tax cuts that make economic sense. A moderate, short-term tax cut could serve as a stimulant to consumer spending and thus prevent the economy from going into a deep recession. I would suggest a one-time tax rebate to every American taxpayer of...

I am enclosing a copy of the video of my eight-minute interview with Lou Waters on CNN and a copy of my 128-page book, *The Alleged Budget Surplus, Social Security, and Voodoo Economics.* Please take the time to view this short interview and read this very short book. I had no plans to write the book until all candidates for the presidency, from both parties, began talking about the nonexistent "budget surplus" during the presidential primaries. I felt it my duty to write the book, and I feel it is my duty to do everything I can to prevent another round of Reaganomics. I would like to have the opportunity to testify before Congressional committees and do anything else that I can do for the cause of economic literacy.

Sincerely,

Allen W. Smith, Ph.D.

P.S. America very much needs your help and that of your colleagues in alerting the public to the fact that they have been deceived into believing there is a budget surplus when, in fact, the government's long-term finances are the worst they have ever been...Your staff can verify every statistic in my book with a couple of hours of research. During my interview with Lou Waters on CNN, he asked me if I was a voice crying in the wilderness. So far, that is pretty much the case. I feel like a modern-day Paul Revere trying to warn my fellow Americans of a forthcoming assault on the U.S. Treasury and the American economy, but because of such widespread economic illiteracy at all levels, almost nobody is hearing the warning. Please check out the economic facts.

I was really pumping adrenaline during that project, and, as I took all those Priority Mail packages to the post office so they could start their journey to Washington, I may have fancied myself as someone like the little Dutch boy who supposedly stuck his thumb in the hole in the dike to prevent a catastrophe.

I felt good about the effort I had made, and I hoped that at least a few senators would read the book and give some thought to my warnings. I knew that I would not hear from many of the senators, but, as the days and weeks passed by without a single reply, I began to feel depressed and a little hopeless. I guess I just wasn't prepared to accept the reality that any professional, in any field, could write 100 letters to United States senators, expressing grave concern about the nation's future, and give away 100 books and videos of a CNN interview on the subject, and still not hear a word from even one senator.

I became discouraged and was considering giving up my crusade in the summer of 2001 when I had an epiphany of sorts while standing in a long line at the post office. I got this crazy idea that maybe if I plastered my 1991 red Oldsmobile Cutlass Supreme car with large signs, warning of impending danger, and drove from city to city, I might get some news coverage for my message. It was totally contrary to my personality and judgment to resort to publicity stunts in a desperate attempt to call attention to myself and my message. But I did it anyway.

I placed signs, warning about budget deficits and Social Security, all over the car. I even attached signs with very large letters to the top of the car in the hope that news organizations with helicopters might come down for a closer look. I then began driving my "debtmobile" throughout the state of Florida. I drove up and down the streets of Miami, Tampa, Tallahassee and other cities.

I was even considering driving the "debtmobile" from Florida to Washington D.C. if early publicity results indicated that such a venture was warranted, but they did not. I got some publicity, but not nearly as much as I had hoped for. The most significant news coverage was in the form of an Associated Press story in early September. Below is a reprint of the AP story.

ECONOMIST WARNED OF BUDGET SURPLUS MYTH, NOW VINDICATED
By Vickie Chachere, Associated Press
(Reprinted with permission of The Associated Press)

TAMPA—A year ago, economist Allen W. Smith seemed an oddity, a bespectacled Chicken Little with an ominous warning that the nation's economic outlook wasn't as good as it seemed.

He wrote a book about what he believes is a myth of a federal budget surplus. He even went on CNN to spread his warnings there was no surplus, only a looming national debt.

Still no one seemed to be listening . Smith, a former writer of an economics column and the author of nine books, pressed on.

The election—with its candidates making big promises about how they would use the surplus—came and went, and Smith grew frustrated.

Finally, two months ago, Smith a Midwesterner not prone to absurd acts, felt moved to plaster signs on his bright red car and drive about town in and elaborate "The End is Near" sort of warning.

Smith's grown children were embarrassed. Some of his neighbors called him a loon.

Then this week came vindication with news the government needs to borrow $9 billion from Social Security reserves to make ends meet, says a new Congressional Budget Office estimate.

"I knew this would happen," said Smith, 63, trying hard not to gloat.

"(CNN's) Lou Waters said I was a voice crying in the wilderness, I guess I was. I knew it was just a matter of time."

If it wasn't such a serious issue, it might almost be comical, but for Smith, a professor emeritus at Eastern Illinois University who has long been on a crusade to educate the common folk about the weighty issues of economics, it's more proof that what Americans don't know about economics hurts them.

"It's a deception they (voters) like to hear," he said. "The problem is the economic illiteracy."

For Smith, the lack of understanding about budget surpluses and deficits is a double concern.

Not only does he feel politicians have been misleading people about how such surpluses could be spent on improved health care or education, he worries that people are making poor choices for themselves based on misinformation. He fears a deep, prolonged economic recession is ahead.

"I actually have a very gloomy outlook," Smith said. "I'm glad I'm retired and not out in the job market."

Smith's book, *The Alleged Budget Surplus, Social Security & Voodoo Economics,* calls the budget surplus a myth that "may go down in history as the greatest deception perpetrated on the American people."

In the book, written in early spring last year, Smith argued that the economy was healthy, but the federal budget was not.

The bulk of the budget surplus was Social Security Trust Fund money and it wasn't the government's to spend on programs other than paying benefits to those who have paid into the retirement program, he wrote. The book was published in late September.

Using data gleaned from the U.S. Department of the Treasury and other government economic reports, Smith argues in his book that the public was duped into believing there was a surplus and is forgetting $5.7 trillion national debt.

He said the only surpluses were in 1999 and 2000, in the peak of the economic boom, and they were smaller than the public was led to believe, Smith contends.

Smith took to task both Republicans and Democrats in the book, calling their comments about the economy and their campaign promises simply irresponsible.

He does, however, think the recent tax rebates are a good idea for a short-term boost for the economy, if they're spent as President Bush intends.

Frustrated by the lack of interest in the issue, Smith said he was ready to give up earlier this summer when he had an epiphany while standing in line at a post office.

Soon thereafter, his cherry red 1991 Oldsmobile Cutlass Supreme was transformed into the debt mobile. Smith plastered the car with signs warning of the $1 billion-a-day interest and the mythical surplus and began traveling the state....

Vickie Chachere, the AP correspondent who wrote the above story, told me that she thought it would be picked up by newspapers around the country. My hopes began to build that my efforts would soon pay off as the budget surplus myth, which Bush was still playing to the hilt, was exposed. I thought it was just a matter of time until the media and the American public would learn that they were being deliberately deceived by their government.

I spoke with Vickie by phone just before the story was to be released to the wires, and I said something like, "I hope there are no major stories that dominate the news and crowd out the other stories." Vickie said she thought things would be relatively quiet and that I needn't worry about the story not receiving wide exposure.

The story appeared on the Florida wire and was about to go national. But, like so many other stories, it was buried by the avalanche of news generated by the events of September 11. To my knowledge, the story never made it to the national wire.

After the terrorist attacks, with the nation at war, support for President Bush surged, and nobody bothered to follow up on Bush's pledge that he would not raid the Social Security trust fund. And, even if he were raiding it in order to pay for the war, most Americans would probably not have had a problem with that. American's have always been willing to make sacrifices during times of war.

But Bush began raiding the trust fund even before the September 11, 2001 terrorist attacks. Fiscal year 2001 ended on September 30, just 19 days after the September 11 attacks, so there was not enough time for any effects to be reflected in that year's budget. Thus, the Social Security lockbox was broken into even before we knew we would be spending a lot of money on war.

Furthermore, in early 2003, at a time when the previous year's non-Social Security deficit had been a whopping $317.5 billion, and every dollar of the Social Security surplus was being spent on general government, Bush called for a second round of tax cuts. Despite a public outcry of protest by economists, Bush pushed through a $330 billion new tax cut in May 2003.

It was extremely frustrating for me to watch Bush spend the Social Security surplus that resulted from contributions of American workers, some of them very poor, and at the same time push through tax cuts for some of the wealthiest Americans. In essence, he was using the Social Security surpluses to fund his tax cuts for the rich.

I continued to try to get this information to the media, but it seemed that, in the minds of most journalists, the trust fund issue had been resolved during the 2000 presidential election campaign. Both Al Gore and George W. Bush had acknowledged at that time that the trust fund had been raided in the past, but both pledged that if elected president they would end the practice. The fact that Bush pledged to protect the Social Security trust fund during speeches, both before and after, becoming president, seemed sufficient to end the public debate.

But Bush did not keep his promise. He raided the trust fund in each and every year of his presidency. In total, President George W. Bush spent $1.37 trillion of Social Security surplus revenue during his eight years as president. In his last year, he spent $192.2 billion, which averages out to more than $526 million per day!

As I continued to try to raise public awareness to the Social Security fraud, I kept hoping that some high-ranking public official would confirm that what I was saying was true. In order to believe my assertion that the Social Security trust fund was empty, the public had to hear it from somebody with clout.

On January 21, 2005, David Walker, the Comptroller General of the Government Accountability

Office (GAO), gave a speech in Washington in which he said,

> "The left hand owes the right hand, and that has legal, political and moral significance. But it doesn't have any economic significance whatsoever. There are no stocks or bonds or real estate in the trust fund. It has nothing of real value to draw down."

I thought a public statement by the Comptroller General of the GAO, saying the trust fund holds no bonds and has nothing of real value to draw down, was just what I needed. But, to my amazement, the statement received very little news coverage. If I hadn't read about Walker's statement in the San Francisco Chronicle, I might have never known about it, because I didn't see it anywhere else.

On April 5, 2005, President George W. Bush made the following statement during a speech at West Virginia University at Parkerburg:

> "There is no trust fund, just IOUs that I saw first-hand that future generations will pay—will pay for either in higher taxes, or reduced benefits, or cuts to other critical government programs."

Once Bush began to repeatedly admit that the government had spent all the Social Security money that was supposed to be in the trust fund, I thought the truth was out for all to see. But even President Bush's repeated public statements that the Social Security trust fund was empty didn't receive much news coverage despite the fact that what he was saying was just the opposite of what he had said earlier.

In his first State of the Union address, delivered on February 27, 2001, President Bush had said,

> "To make sure the retirement savings of America's seniors are not diverted in any other program, my budget protects all $2.6 trillion of the Social Security surplus for Social Security, and for Social Security alone."

The very next day, the Office of Management and Budget had released the following statement,

> "None of the Social Security trust funds and Medicare trust funds will be used to fund other spending initiatives or tax relief."

These statements, and several others made by Bush early in his presidency, are totally contradictory to his contention in 2005 that the trust fund contained nothing but IOUs. At first, I thought that my efforts to convince the public that the government was spending the Social Security surplus money just as if it were general revenue, and that the trust fund was empty, were no longer needed. The President of the United States had just done my job for me. But it didn't work out that way. Nobody seemed to take Bush seriously once he began to actually tell the truth about Social Security. The public still seemed convinced that all the surplus money that had been paid into the Social Security trust fund was safe and sound.

I began to feel much like Australian physician, Dr. Barry Marshall, must have felt for more than a decade. In the early 1980s, Dr. Marshall discovered a link between a certain bacteria and peptic ulcers. His early research led him to believe that ulcers were caused by this bacteria, and that patients with this bacteria were also at significant risk for developing stomach cancer. If his belief that peptic ulcers were caused by bacteria was correct, this meant that ulcers might be cured with antibiotics.

However, since medical students had been taught for decades that ulcers were caused by excess stomach acid, and because treatment of stomach acid had become a big industry, there was much organized resistance to Dr. Marshall's findings. He was ridiculed by fellow professionals and by pharmaceutical companies. Among other things, he was called a "crazy man saying crazy things." In 1998, by which time his treatment for ulcers had become almost universally accepted, he was quoted as saying "Everyone was against me, but I knew I was right." During the decade it took for the medical profession to accept Dr. Barry Marshall's findings, many patients throughout the world suffered needlessly, and some even died, from an ailment for which a cure had been found.

Another example of the preventable suffering of thousands of people resulted from the now infamous Bernard Madoff Ponzi scheme. Madoff, a former chairman of the Nasdaq Stock Market, and a widely respected Wall Street trader, was arrested by federal agents after admitting that he had swindled clients out of approximately $50 billion. Over a period of many years, Madoff had ripped off investors from around the world including many large charitable organizations.

It was only after Madoff's arrest that the public learned that a man named Harry Markopolos had been trying to expose Madoff's fraud for nine years. Markopolos, with the help of a mathematician, concluded in 1999 that Madoff's operation could not be legitimate. Using data that Madoff's firm distributed to prospective investors, Markopolos and the mathematician concluded within hours that it was impossible for Madoff to get the returns he reported while using the strategy he said he used. Markopolos informed the SEC's Boston office in May 1999 that it was impossible for the kind of profit Madoff was reporting to have been gained legally. But the SEC was not interested in Markopolos's theory. Madoff continued to thrive, and Markopolos continued to pursue the case.

In 2005, Markopolos submitted a report to the SEC saying it was "highly likely" that Madoff securities is the world's largest Ponzi scheme." But the report was not taken seriously.

Markopolos continued to pursue the case for a total of nine years up until the time Madoff was arrested. Had the SEC listened to Markopolos in 1999, thousands of individuals and organizations would have avoided being swindled out of billions of dollars.

Coincidentally, nine years is how long I have been persistently trying to alert the public to the Social Security fraud. During the nine years since I first began trying to alert the public to the fact that all surplus Social Security revenue is being fraudulently spent on other government programs, more than $1.37 trillion has been looted and spent. That money, which belonged to the Social Security trust fund, and to American workers who had made Social Security contributions through the payroll tax, is gone, and the government continues to loot and spend more than $500 million of additional Social Security money each and every day.

Why has it been so difficult to alert the public to the fact that the Social Security trust fund contains no real assets? Why is it so hard for the public to accept the fact that the government has looted the trust fund of every penny of the surplus Social Security tax revenue and spent the money on other things?

I think that part of the problem is the fact that conservative organizations, such as the Cato Institute and the Heritage Foundation, have been trying for decades to destroy the current Social Security system and replace it with a private system. As we saw in Chapter Five, the Bush privatization campaign was based on the strategy set forth in 1983 by this movement.

The strategy of the privatizers is to convince the public that the current Social Security system is unsustainable in the long run and that it should be replaced with a system of private accounts. Among the many arguments of this group has been that the Social Security trust fund contains no real assets—only IOUs. Therefore, when anyone suggests that the trust fund is empty, the ardent defenders of the current system automatically assume that the critic is a privatizer who is trying to destroy the current Social Security system.

I am not such a person. I am strongly opposed to any attempt to privatize Social Security. What I have been trying to do is to save the current Social

Security system by exposing the fraudulent raiding of the trust fund by the government.

I believe that Social Security is the most successful and most popular program ever created by the United States government. It has lifted millions of Americans out of poverty and made their final years tolerable, if not golden. Social Security has worked well for the past 70 years, and it can work well for the next 70 years and beyond, if it is put on, and kept on, a solid foundation. Those people who dislike Social Security do so for ideological and political reasons—not because the program is unworkable or unsustainable.

There is nothing fundamentally wrong with the current structure of the Social Security program. The short-term funding problems with Social Security are the result of the government's "borrowing" and spending the Social Security surplus funds for more than two decades. Despite the claims and counter claims of various groups and individuals, President Bush was correct when he said there are no real assets in the trust fund. He was also correct when he said that, beginning in 2017, when Social Security begins to run annual deficits, it will not be able to pay full benefits unless the government raises taxes, borrows additional amounts from the public, or cuts government spending.

As we saw in Chapter 3, the main point of confusion on this whole matter seems to be that most people don't understand that public issue, marketable Treasury bonds are something very different from the non-marketable special issue government IOUs that are held by the Social Security trust fund.

The key to understanding what is going on is to keep your eye on the money. If the government bought public- issue bonds in the open market, the money would go to the party selling the bonds, and none of it would be available for the government to spend. This would be a true investment. However, the special issue certificates allow the government to keep and spend all the money. Since the money is all spent, there is nothing left to invest. But the government has met the letter of the law by printing up a certificate that says "backed by the full faith and credit of the United States government."

In addition to the role that conservative organizations have played in blocking my message, the 35-million-member AARP has made my task of informing the public about the Social Security fraud much more difficult. They have continued to insist that the Social Security trust fund holds bonds that are just like the ones held by private pension funds, insurance companies and most other investors, "*because they are the safest investment in the world.*"

I don't know whether the AARP leadership is so naïve that they actually believe what they are saying, or whether they have other motives for helping to hide the Social Security fraud from the public. What I do know is that they have rejected my extensive efforts to get them involved in helping to alert the public about the fact that the Social Security surplus money has all been spent and there are no real assets in the trust fund. Even though I was a member of the AARP for many years, the leadership seemed to view me and my message as a threat to their agenda. I am not sure why.

On July 18, 2004 the *St. Petersburg Times* published an article entitled "Social Security Assessments Clash" written by personal finance editor, Helen Huntley. Ms. Huntley had submitted four questions on Social Security to both AARP Chief Executive, William Novelli and to me. The first question was about the trust fund. That portion of the article is presented below as it appeared in the *Times.*

Q: Is the Social Security trust fund a fraud?

Smith: The concept of the Social Security trust fund is not a fraud, but the looting of the fund by the government is, in my opinion, the greatest fraud ever perpetrated on the American people by their government.

Prior to 1983, Social Security operated on a pay-as-you-go principle with an approximately balanced budget most years. However, in 1982 a presidential commission headed by Alan Greenspan was given the task of studying the long-term solvency of the program and making recommendations for the future. The commission concluded that the only way Social Security would be able to fund the retirement of the baby boom generation, beginning in about 2010, would be to raise taxes and build up a reserve in advance of retirement. In 1983 Congress passed, and the president signed, the legislation recommended by the Greenspan commission. Taxes were raised and the money was supposed to be specifically earmarked for the funding of the baby boomers' retirement. Approximately $1.5 trillion of Social Security revenue has been generated by the tax increase so far and should be available when the baby boomers retire.

Here is where the fraud begins. Every dollar of that surplus has been borrowed, embezzled, stolen by the government and used for other spending programs and to finance tax cuts. The money from the trust fund has been replaced with essentially worthless government

IOUs that are not marketable and cannot be used to pay benefits.

Novelli: Absolutely not! Social Security has always had a trust fund in which all revenues (tax receipts and interest) to pay Social Security benefits are deposited and from which all benefits are paid. The law requires that any surplus revenues not immediately needed to pay benefits have to be invested in U.S. Treasury bonds. Currently, the Social Security trust fund holds more than $1.5 trillion of Treasury bonds that earn interest. These bonds are like the ones bought by private pension funds, insurance companies and individuals because they are the safest investment in the world.

   Some people claim that the Treasury bonds owned by Social Security are worthless IOUs and that the Social Security trust fund is in trouble. But they are wrong. Investors worldwide know that the U.S. government has always paid every penny of interest and principal on Treasury bonds when they are due and will continue to do so. Just as Social Security has never missed a single monthly benefit payment, Treasury bonds have always been paid in full and on time.

When Novelli said, "These bonds are like the ones bought by private pension funds, insurance companies and individuals because they are the safest investment in the world," he was totally wrong. Novelli appeared to be talking about public-issue Treasury bonds which are probably the safest investment in the world. These are the type of bonds that the Social Security surplus should have been invested in because they are good-as-gold, default-proof, securities.

   Unfortunately, not a single dollar of the Social Security surplus is invested in public-issue Treasury bonds. The special-issue IOUs that the trust fund holds were created specifically for the trust funds, and they are held only by the trust funds.

Private pension funds and other investors could not invest in the special-issue IOUs, even if they wanted to. However, no outside investor would touch these IOU's with a ten-foot pole because they are worthless.

As I have stated many times in this book, the Social Security surplus funds were not invested in anything. All of the money was spent by the government on other programs, so there was nothing left to invest. What the Treasury does when it spends Social Security money on other programs is to create IOU's to serve as accounting records of the money "borrowed" from Social Security.

Prior to 1994, the IOUs consisted only of accounting entries recorded in government ledgers or stored on computers. However, some members of Congress began to worry that someone might want to actually see the IOUs, so legislation was passed that required the physical printing of documents to serve as certificates of indebtedness, in addition to the accounting entry. Today, when a new IOU is issued, it is printed on a laser printer located at the Bureau of the Public Debt office in Parkersburg, West Virginia. Once printed, the document is carried across the room and placed in a fireproof filing cabinet. That filing cabinet is the closest thing to the mythical Social Security trust fund that exists.

EPILOGUE

The Case For Universal
Economic Education

*A government resting upon popular suffrage cannot be
successful unless those who elect and who obey their
government are educated.*—John Dewey

This book describes how political leaders have
managed to knowingly and deliberately inflict great
harm on the economy, the federal budget, and the
American people by pursuing policies that were in-
compatible with sound principles of economics.
During the 12 years of the Reagan-Bush administrations, the national debt quadrupled, and by the time
George H.W. Bush turned over the powers of the
presidency to Bill Clinton in January 1993, the
economy and the federal budget were headed for a
crash.

Economists, who had seen the calamity coming
since the early days of the Reagan administration,
breathed a sigh of relief when George H.W. Bush
was forced to step aside and turn the controls over
to Clinton, but many economists had serious doubts
that Clinton could avert the crash at that late stage
of the downward plunge. However, with the help of

a crew made up of some of the most competent economists available, the crash was averted, and the plane known as the American economy began to recover altitude. If the new pilot had not been capable of understanding what the economists were saying, or if he had failed to implement their advice, there is little doubt that the crash would have come on Clinton's watch.

Fortunately, Clinton was able to see the impending crisis. He took the corrective actions recommended by the economists, which included both major spending cuts and a tax increase. He was opposed by every single Republican member of both the House and the Senate, and he managed to get the urgently needed legislation through Congress only with the tie-breaking vote of Vice President Al Gore. Many of Clinton's opponents predicted that his policies would devastate the economy. They argued that the new pilot would crash the plane by following the advice of his trusted economists, especially the advice to raise income taxes. Specifically, Senator Robert Dole said, "To put it simply, the Clinton tax increase promises to turn the American dream into a nightmare for millions of hard-working Americans."

The critics were wrong. The economy responded to the new policies remarkable well. The downward plunge was aborted, and the plane began at first to level off, and then to resume its upward journey once again. Economists were relieved, and soon the skills of the new pilot were publicly recognized by experts. Former Federal Reserve chairmen, Paul Volker and Alan Greenspan, both praised Clinton's piloting skills as did many other prominent public figures. It seemed that the only ones who were displeased with the results of Clinton's piloting were the Republicans, who had made a big deal back in 1993 about how they did not want to be held responsible for the consequences of Clinton's economic policies.

Most fair-minded Americans did not hold the Republicans responsible, nor did they give them any credit for the prosperity and diminishing deficits that resulted from Clinton's policies. How could they be held responsible when not a single one of them had voted for the program.

The American economy was soaring at a high altitude by the end of Clinton's presidency. The economy was in the tenth year of the longest expansion in history, the unemployment rate was at a 30-year low, and we had just experienced the first two years of true budget surpluses in 38 years. But it was time for the pilot, who had averted the near crash, and now had the economy soaring, to step aside. The new pilot was a student of Reaganomics, who was also the son of the man who had almost crashed the economy before Clinton came along just in the nick of time.

Economists listened to George W. Bush's plan with alarm. He was proposing to undo what had been accomplished during the previous eight years. He was calling for another round of Reaganomics, the policy that had almost caused the economy to crash before Clinton took charge.

The national debt was more than $6 trillion when George W. Bush became president, so it was absolutely shocking when the new pilot proposed additional large cuts in tax rates. The tax rate structure that existed after the Clinton tax increase was still unable to generate enough revenue to balance the budget except in those last two Clinton years when the economy was operating at the very top of the business cycle. There had been deficits during 6 of the 8 years that Clinton had occupied the White House so, as soon as the economy slipped into even a minor recession, the nation was bound to experience at least small annual budget deficits under the tax structure that George W. Bush inherited from Clinton.

If Bush had left tax rates alone, and worked to cut government spending as much as possible, we might have had almost balanced budgets in the years ahead, and the economy could have continued to prosper. But that was not the route that Bush took. He advocated massive tax cuts. Had he learned nothing from the policies of Reagan and his father! This new daredevil pilot was preparing to throw the economy back into a nosedive. But how could he? Didn't he realize just how close we had come to crashing before his father was relieved of his duties? And, if he did realize the close call America had had before Clinton took office, was he out of his mind to propose another crash attempt? It just didn't make sense to economists, and, if the people had understood what George W. Bush was up to, they would probably have refused to support him. But they did not understand.

Many were concerned that what Bush was proposing lacked the support of most professionally trained economists, but Bush convinced them that he knew more than the economists knew. Most

Americans did not have a clue that Bush was lying to them when he made the following statements:

> "My plan pays down an unprecedented amount of our national debt."

> "My budget protects all $2.6 trillion of the Social Security surplus for Social Security and for Social Security alone."

> "And then, when money is still left over, my plan returns it to the people who earned it in the first place."

Even if there had been no tax cuts, there would not have been any money with which to pay down the debt by even one dollar during Bush's term unless he either raised taxes or cut government spending in other areas. Even during the prosperous Clinton years, only during his last two years in office, when the economy was at the peak of the business cycle, was there any surplus money that could be used to pay down the national debt. There was little likelihood that there would be any non-Social Security surpluses in the years ahead, no matter who was serving as president.

And, just as there was no money to pay down the debt, there was also not a single dollar available for funding tax cuts. The only way that Bush could have cut taxes without damaging the economy and the budget would have been to cut government spending dollar for dollar by the amount of any tax cut. But this was not what the voters wanted to hear. So Bush chose to tell them that he would pay down the debt, protect Social Security money, and also cut taxes. He knew he was lying to the American people, but it didn't seem to bother him.

As I pointed out earlier in this book, Bill Clinton, Al Gore, and many members of Congress from both parties also lied about the existence of a mythical government surplus. They should also be condemned for their lies, but the fact that others had lied did not justify, or excuse, Bush's lies and actions. How could the president of the United States blatantly lie to the American people in his State of the Union address about an issue that was so crucial to our economic security? I can't answer that question. All I know is that George W. Bush did lie to the American people about the financial condition of the government in his 2001 State of the Union address, and he continued to lie about the economy and the federal budget throughout his presidency.

Of all the lies Bush told, I personally find the lie that the 2003 tax cut was a jobs-creation program the most offensive, and the most cruel, of all. More than two million Americans lost their jobs between the time of Bush's inauguration and his last-minute campaign to muster enough votes in Congress to pass the 2003 tax cuts.

As I stated earlier, 400 of the nation's top economists, including 10 who had won the Nobel prize in economics, were so concerned about the damage the tax cut would do, that they placed a full-page ad in the *New York Times* in an effort to get their message to the public. The economists stated in their ad that the purpose of the Bush tax cut was "a permanent change in the tax structure and not the creation of jobs and growth in the near-term."

It is hard to understand how any president of the United States could do what Bush did in those last few days before the tax cut was passed. He totally ignored the warnings of these top experts and set out to convince the people that his bill would do just the opposite of what the 400 experts had said it would do. Few people outside New York City were aware of the economists' statement, and Bush wanted to keep it that way. He went on a speaking blitz to drum up votes for passage of his bill. In speech after speech, he referred to the high unemployment in America and claimed that his tax cut was a solution to it. He referred to the bill over and over as a "jobs-creation" program that must be passed in order to solve the problem of high unemployment.

Every time he made that statement, he knew he was deliberately lying to the people who had put so much trust in him. He didn't try to refute the economists' argument that the tax cut would not create many jobs. Instead, he took advantage of the fact that most Americans were totally unaware of the economists' warning. Most Americans could not have imagined that the "trustworthy" President George W. Bush would be pushing any kind of legislation that was opposed by the vast majority of experts in the field. Most thought Bush was trying to do something good for them by pushing through legislation that would reduce unemployment.

The nation very much needed a real jobs-creation bill at that time, and the cost of a true jobs-creation program would have been only a fraction of the cost of Bush's big tax cut for the rich. For example, a bill that would have provided for the sending of a one-time check of $1,000 to every American taxpayer would have given the economy a real big jolt—perhaps even too big a jolt—but it would not have changed tax rates and would therefore not have contributed significantly to long-term budget deficits. Economists would have gladly supported such a measure with the amount of the rebate adjusted to the level that would have provided the appropriate boost to the economy.

Bush could have easily gotten such legislation through and could have made a major contribution toward putting unemployed workers back to work. Instead, he chose to do another big favor for members of his own socioeconomic class—the people who had made possible his presidency and who would finance his reelection campaign. Bush knew that every favor he did for these people would make it easier for him to raise massive amounts of money with which to "buy" a second term. A few weeks after passage of the 2003 tax cut, Bush raised $7 million in campaign contributions during one weekend in Texas. Such campaign contributions by the wealthy to the first Bush campaign probably yielded a greater return to the donors than any other investment they had ever made.

My first book, *Understanding Inflation and Unemployment,* which was published in 1976, was written because of my frustration with President Lyndon B. Johnson's failure to follow sound economic policies. Johnson failed to head off the terrible inflation that was triggered at least partly by the massive increase in spending on the Vietnam war without a corresponding increase in taxes. That book marked the beginning of my long crusade for economic education to combat the incredibly dangerous economic illiteracy of the American people.

Later, I was absolutely dumbfounded by Reagan's economic proposals—the ones that George H.W. Bush initially called "voodoo economics." I was even more shocked when Reagan's proposals were enacted into law, and America started down the long road toward economic disaster.

It was like a huge breath of fresh air when Bill Clinton was elected and began once again implementing sound economic policies. Because of the success of Clinton's policies, and the contrast between the results of his economic policies and those of Ronald Reagan and George H.W. Bush, I allowed myself to hope that major economic malpractice might be a thing of the past.

Americans could clearly see how different the 12 years under Reagan-Bush were as compared to the 8 years of Clinton when traditional economic policies were again followed. Very few Americans would say that they were better off under Reagan-Bush than under Clinton. There had never been greater economic prosperity in America than during the last two years of the Clinton presidency.

In my mind, it didn't matter all that much whether a Democrat or a Republican succeeded Clinton, because the value of following the advice of highly competent economic advisers had been demonstrated. Surely, even a Republican president would follow sound economic policies, I thought. And I still believe that most of the other Republican candidates for president in 2000 would have followed sound economic policies. Certainly John McCain would have done so.

But, George W. Bush was the one who made it
to the White House, and he followed through with
his radical economic policies that were so unthinkable to many economists. He was determined to
push through his big tax cuts for the wealthy, come
hell or high water, and there was nothing anybody
could do to stop him, given the high degree of economic illiteracy in America.

All the economic malpractice of the past, and the
suffering that has resulted from it, could have been
avoided if the American public had been economically literate. But they are not. They are incredibly
illiterate on the subject of economics. This applies
to highly educated professionals just as much as it
does to the general public, and it especially applies
to all government officials. I seriously doubt that
George W. Bush, or most members of Congress,
could pass a basic economic literacy test.

Most Americans have never formally studied
economics. Only 17 states require that high school
students take a course on basic economics and the
American economy. As a result, most high school
graduates have never been exposed to the subject.
In many of the nation's high schools, economics is
not even offered as an elective course for those students who might want to take it.

One of the most powerful actions that our government could take to reduce economic illiteracy,
and thus economic malpractice, in the long run,
would be to ensure that every future high school
graduate will have taken a course on the American
economy before being allowed to graduate. While
the federal government might not have the authority
to mandate what is taught in the individual states, it

could certainly use the carrot and stick approach. If the government adopted a policy of withholding federal education funds from any school that did not teach a required course on the American economy, almost every high school in the nation would soon be teaching the subject.

The cost of adding a course on the American economy would be minimal for most high schools. Every licensed high school social studies teacher has already had some training in economics, and the National Council on Economic Education, through its local centers for economic education, offers special classes designed to train high school teachers to teach economics. Seventeen states have already shouldered the responsibility of educating students on the American economy. We can't wait decades for the other states to follow in their footsteps. We must take action now to ensure that the next generation will not be as economically illiterate as the present one is.

If the current generation of Americans had been well educated in economics, the 2008 meltdown almost certainly would not have happened. It was only the economic illiteracy of the people that allowed the gross economic malpractice by our government over the past quarter-century. A literate public would never have supported the 2003 tax cut once they learned that 400 of the nation's top economists were screaming out warnings against the dangerous legislation.

Requiring every future high school graduate to have taken a course on the American economy is a good starting point, but it is not nearly enough. I believe the government should sponsor free adult night classes at community colleges and local high schools for the members of the general public who would like to learn about the American economy.

Some people think that those with a college education surely must know a great deal about the economy as well as most other subjects, but that is not true. The majority of college graduates are economically illiterate, having made it through college without taking a single course in economics. In most colleges, economics is not a general education requirement. Only students with certain majors are required to take it as part of their college education.

As a result, there are many doctors, lawyers, and other highly educated individuals who have almost no understanding of the American economy. Like the public in general, from which they come, most members of the United States Congress have probably never had any formal training in economics. Yet they play a major role in the functioning of the economy through the legislation they pass. It is very much like the blind leading the blind. A president, who knows little about economics, proposes basic legislation that will have a major impact on the economy and the future of the American people. An equally illiterate Congress then debates the proposed legislation, almost exclusively along ideological and political lines, because they don't know enough to debate the economic aspects of the legislation. In addition, if competent economists try to point out flaws in the legislation, they are almost always ignored as irrelevant.

Educators in almost all disciplines think that their discipline should be more widely taught. One person even raised the following question to me.

"Why should all students be required to take economics unless they are also required to take chemistry?" My response to this type of argument is that the American voters are rarely called upon to vote on issues that require a good understanding of chemistry. In such fields we can rely on the experts to keep us on the right track. But every time voters vote, economic issues are involved, and our government has a terrible track record in terms of its willingness to listen to professionally trained economists.

Every high school student gets instruction in both American history and American government, but most do not study the American economy. Yet, it is not possible to have a good understanding of either American history or American government without also having a good understanding of the American economy. It may not be necessary for people who live in non-democratic countries to be educated in economics, since they don't have any say in government policies. But it is absolutely essential that those of us who live in America have at least some familiarity with economics and the American economy.

When President George W. Bush ignored the warnings of the nation's top economists and pushed through his dangerously irresponsible 2003 tax cut, it removed any remaining doubt that professional economists might have had that they could have an impact on economic policy-making. It is absolutely crucial that we Americans try to protect ourselves, and the nation, against radical economic malpractice by becoming more informed about the American economy.

I urge readers to support universal economic education at the high school level, and to try to persuade colleges and universities to make principles of economics a general education requirement so that at least college graduates will be able to play a role in battling economic malpractice. I also urge readers to support the creation of a national economic advisory council similar to the one I proposed in the previous chapter. The American people need a watchdog agency to protect them from government officials like President George W. Bush who attempt to exploit economic illiteracy in order to further their partisan political agendas.

INDEX

DATE DUE

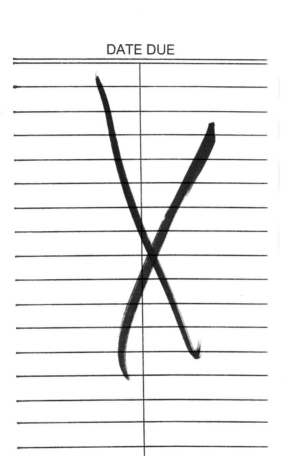

DEMCO, INC. 38-2931